# Corpora in Translator Education

Edited by

## FEDERICO ZANETTIN, SILVIA BERNARDINI AND DOMINIC STEWART

*Karen Scojo*

ST JEROME
PUBLISHING

St. Jerome Publishing
Manchester, UK & Northampton MA

Published by
St. Jerome Publishing
2 Maple Road West, Brooklands
Manchester, M23 9HH, United Kingdom
Tel +44 161 973 9856
Fax +44 161 905 3498
stjerome@compuserve.com
http://www.stjerome.co.uk

ISBN 1-900650-60-6 (pbk)

Printed and bound in Great Britain by
T. J. International Ltd., Cornwall, UK

Typeset by
Delta Typesetters, Cairo, Egypt
Email: hilali1945@hotmail.com

*British Library Cataloguing in Publication Data*
A catalogue record of this book is available from the British Library

*Library of Congress Cataloging-in-Publication Data*
Corpora in translator education / edited by Federico Zanettin, Silvia Bernardini, and Dominic Stewart.
    p. cm.
  ISBN 1-900650-60-6 (Paperback : alk. paper)
 1. Translating and interpreting--Study and teaching (Higher)--Data processing. I. Zanettin, Federico. II. Bernardini, Silvia. III. Stewart, Dominic.
  P306.5.C67 2003
  418'.02'0711--dc21
                                    2003010199

# Contents

# Corpora in Translator Education

## An Introduction

SILVIA BERNARDINI
DOMINIC STEWART
FEDERICO ZANETTIN

## 1. Applied corpus-based translation studies

Language corpora, i.e. principled collections of texts in electronic format, are increasingly being used as a resource in linguistics and
language-related disciplines, and corpus linguistics is now firmly established as a research area and a methodology. One of the many fields where
corpora are having a growing impact is translation, both at a descriptive
and a practical level. This book is principally concerned with the use of
corpora as resources for the translator and as teaching/learning aids in the
context of the translation classroom – an area which could be termed "applied corpus-based translation studies" in terms of the 'map' of translation
studies first proposed by Holmes in ((1972) 1988) and later elaborated by
a number or scholars, notably Toury (1995).

The last decade of the twentieth century saw an unprecedented growth
of public and private institutions devoted to the training, or, better, *education*, of translators and interpreters throughout Europe and the world
(Caminade and Pym 1995). The papers in this volume, which grew out of
presentations at the CULT2K Conference[1], record work in progress in
some of the liveliest among these institutions. Though the case studies
reported and activities proposed reflect curricula that vary according to
local educational characteristics, the learning contexts they address are in
many ways similar. Such institutions rarely know for certain whether their
students will work for large governmental translation agencies, as free-
lance literary translators, as interpreters, or as language service providers
in some other capacity, and teaching them to translate usually goes hand-
in-hand with perfecting their working languages. The use of corpora in
these contexts stands at the interface between translation and language

---

[1]The second *Conference on Corpus Use and Learning to Translate* took place in
Bertinoro, Italy, in November 2000. See Bernardini and Zanettin (2000) for a selection of papers from the previous CULT Conference (1997). Several papers are also
available online http://www.sslmit.unibo.it/cultpaps/paps.htm.

teaching/learning, the expectation being that competent use of corpora and corpus analysis tools will enable students to become better language professionals in a working environment where computational facilities for processing text have become the rule rather than the exception.

From this perspective the papers in this volume make, we believe, an important collective statement at a moment when applied corpus-based translation studies are finally becoming established as a framework for research and pedagogy. Like corpus linguistics a few years ago, they can now be said to have come of age (Svartvik 1992), and signs of this newly-attained maturity abound in this collection. Here we shall draw readers' attention to those features we consider particularly central to the way this field of study is progressing, focussing on how they converge or diverge from such related areas as descriptive corpus-based translation studies, computer-aided translation, and corpus-based language teaching.

## 2.   Translator education at the interface

### 2.1  Corpus-based translation studies

In descriptive translation studies, corpus-based approaches have been used to investigate whether and how translations differ from their source texts, or from original texts written in the target language, and how specific languages and genres as well as translators' stylistic preferences affect translations. Beginning in the early 1990s (following Baker 1993), work in this area has drawn on and brought together aims and methods from descriptive translation studies (cf. Toury 1995) and descriptive corpus linguistics (cf. Sinclair 1991). Translations are seen as subject to socio-cultural norms which are manifested intertextually: the latter can thus be identified through an empirical approach which focuses on the detection and analysis of systematic features of translations in the context of the receiving cultures. Corpus linguistics, as a methodology which focuses on the identification of recurrent patterns of linguistic behaviour in actual performance data, provides the appropriate tool to test hypotheses about norms and regularities in translated texts. Given its emphasis on the target side of translation, work within this paradigm has concentrated on comparable target language corpora, i.e. collections of translated texts and of original texts in the same language (e.g. Laviosa 1997, Olohan and Baker 2000), as well as on parallel or translational corpora, i.e. collections of translated texts and of their source texts in another language (e.g.

Øverås 1998, Kenny 2001).

Descriptive corpus-based translation studies have led to a better understanding of translation phenomena, and helped raise awareness of what is involved in translating. These insights can benefit not only literary translators and translation theorists, but also scholars in related fields (cf. Malmkjær this volume). For reasons that we hope are illustrated by this volume, translator education too can profit from empirically-based discussions of these theoretical and descriptive issues.

## 2.2 Computer-aided translation tools

The influence of corpora has been felt not only in the field of translation description, but also in the more practice-oriented area of professional translator support. Virtually all translators in the Western world now use computers in their everyday work, and process texts electronically. At the same time, research in natural language processing, language engineering and machine translation has been spurred by technological developments, in particular the advent of personal computers and the Internet. As a consequence, translators and other language service providers have access to a wide range of computational resources. They can exploit a vast arrray of electronic reference tools, such as on and off line mono- and bilingual dictionaries and term banks, as well as the largest multimedia encyclopaedia in existence, i.e. the Web. They can obtain real-time help and support from fellow translators through mailing lists and newsgroups. And they can exploit dedicated software suites known as Computer Assisted Translation (CAT) Tools or Translator Workbenches, that combine a text processor with a system for managing 'translation memories' (effectively, a parallel corpus of source texts and their translations) and, optionally, other tools such as a terminology management system, a 'proper' machine translation system, etc. In this last regard, we can note the growing interest in example-based MT systems, partly as a result of the influence of corpus linguistics, which offer promising alternatives to 'traditional' rule-based MT systems (Somers 1998).

Such resources are clearly relevant to the education of prospective translators. It will be an advantage for any future language professional to be skilled in managing state-of-the-art reference tools and translation software, and in integrating different types of computational and managerial resources in the workflow. The emphasis here is generally on non-literary, technical translation, particularly localization and translation in the social services sector – an area in which McEnery and Baker's contribution to this volume highlights the importance of multilingual corpus tools. But we should not be deceived into thinking that technology is the exclusive province of the 'technical' translator. A working knowledge of CAT tools is nowadays in high demand, and is likely to become necessary for all language service providers in the near future.

## 2.3 Corpora in language teaching and learning

The uses of corpora in translation teaching contexts are not limited to translation classes proper, where corpus work can be relevant prior, during or after a translation task (Aston 2000). Corpora can also be used in other courses forming part of the curriculum of translation students, such as second language learning (Bernardini 2000) and terminology (Pearson 1998), and such work can complement translation activities in the narrow sense, developing capacities and competences that are far from marginal to translator education.

The use of corpora in language learning contexts was pioneered by Tim Johns, who introduced concordancing into the foreign language classroom in the 1980s. Besides enabling language professionals such as lexicographers and material writers to produce better reference and learning materials, and allowing language teachers to create classroom activities based on real examples, he showed how corpora could provide learners with direct access to virtually unlimited language data. His methodology of *data-driven learning* (Johns 1991) is a corpus-inspired approach to language pedagogy where learners are encouraged to develop their own hypotheses about textual data and to devise their own strategies for extracting information from corpora. This view of *learning as discovery* seems equally applicable to translator education, and can be found in a number of the papers in this volume. Anna Frankenberg-Garcia and Diane Santos, for instance, present exercises in which learners query parallel texts in the *Compara* corpus in order to highlight the variety of strategies adopted by professional translators and the socio-cultural norms guiding their behaviour (Toury 1995). This approach to parallel concordancing seems to have much in common with Johns' experiment in 'reciprocal learning' (Johns 1997). Here, pairs of British and French students discuss parallel concordances derived from an English-French (non-directional) corpus, and help each other to infer generalisations about specific lexico-grammatical differences between the two languages.

Yet the points of contact between translator education and discovery learning are much more general than this example may suggest. Many of the papers in this volume report on classroom experiences, fulfilling different purposes and using different corpora in different ways. What they have in common is the involvement of learners, who are required to take an active part in their learning process: collecting texts, evaluating corpora, extracting terminology, establishing translational and cross-linguistic equivalences and so on. Learners are not set contrived tasks, whose solutions are artificially kept from them. They solve real problems in authentic situations (or ones perceived as such), often pursuing their own interests, under the guidance of an expert (the teacher). This approach is in line with current views on the value of autonomy, motivation and authenticity in language teaching (Bernardini 2000), as well as with current theories of translator education as a process of socialisation in a professional community (Kiraly 2000).

## 3. The changing field of corpus-based translator education

### 3.1 Corpus typology

A question that crops up throughout this volume regards corpus typology. What corpora are currently being used, constructed, or deemed necessary for translation purposes? Even within the relatively restricted current literature, the reader will find references to monolingual, bilingual, comparable, parallel, monodirectional, bidirectional, reciprocal, virtual, do-it-yourself (DIY), general (large), specialized (small), and reference (very large) corpora.

Probably the most familiar of these are monolingual corpora (whether general or specialized, usually in the target language), comparable bilingual corpora (originals in two languages, selected according to analogous criteria such as topic and text type), and parallel corpora (originals in one language and their translations in another)[2]. The (more or less implicit)

---

[2] As often pointed out, terminology in this area is not consistent. The term 'parallel' has been used to indicate both those corpora we refer to here as 'comparable' (similar originals from two languages) and those we refer to as 'parallel' (originals and their translations). The latter type have also been called "translational" corpora. We hope that the consistent use of these terms in this volume (following the suggestions of Sinclair 1996, Véronis 2000, Kenny 2001) may contribute to greater terminological agreement.

assumptions concerning the uses of these tools are as follows:

- **Monolingual corpora** can provide information about typical 'units of meaning' in the target language or in a specialized subset of it (restricted by topic and/or text type). They can thus help (future) translators opt for natural, 'native-like' turns of phrase, appropriate to the communicative situation in which the target text will be operating. These motivations are similar to those put forward for the use of monolingual corpora in second language learning. Trainee translators are, when translating into their second language, in a position which is very similar to that of L2 learners. As well as learning to translate, they are also learning a second language for a specific purpose, i.e., that of becoming better translators.
- **Comparable bilingual corpora** can provide (future) translators with a better understanding not only of target but also of source texts, allowing them to compare terminology, phraseology and textual conventions across languages and cultures. While monolingual corpora can be large and general, bilingual comparable corpora are usually small and specialized.
- **Parallel corpora** may again be general or specialized, offering learners the possibility to observe what strategies translators appear to privilege, for instance how situationally-constrained expressions are typically translated (cf. Pearson, this volume) or how lexical creativity is dealt with in translation (Kenny 2001). When used in conjunction with monolingual source and target corpora, a parallel corpus can also allow learners to compare features of texts produced under the constraint of translation with 'original' texts in both languages – an opportunity which may also be provided, in principle, by the use of two sets of parallel corpora containing source texts and translations in opposite directions. This latter combination is known as a bidirectional parallel, or reciprocal, corpus.

A number of contributors to this volume, however, discuss corpora that do not fully conform to these categories, or suggest other uses for them. Lynne Bowker and Peter Bennison describe what they prefer to term an *archive* – rather than a corpus – *of student translations*, and the uses this may be put to. Besides lending itself to comparative studies of many sorts (longitudinal analyses of learners' progress, analyses of source language or text-type effects, and so forth), this would also suggest itself as a valuable classroom resource. Like learner language corpora (Granger 1998), learner translation corpora can highlight the inherent intertextuality of discourse, allowing learners to observe their own performance from different angles. They can, for instance, evaluate their strategies in coping with different topics or genres, or observe their progress over time. These activities of immediate relevance to learners can further encourage them to compare their work with that of professional translators, thus making classroom use of better established resources like parallel, comparable and reference corpora more appealing and relevant to them. As claimed by Seidlhofer:

> starting from what learners have said, not just what they might, should or must not say ensures the consideration of two equally crucial points of reference for learners: where they are [...] and where they eventually (may) want to get to [...]. Foregrounding the learners' own criteria of relevance helps negotiate the route between the two, rather than simply displaying the rather remote target behaviour [...]. (Seidlhofer 2000: 222)

This claim seems equally applicable to the use of learner corpora in translator education.

Krista Varantola's paper reports the findings of a workshop experiment using so-called '*disposable corpora*' (also known as virtual, *ad hoc*, and DIY web corpora) – small specialized corpora assembled ad hoc for the purpose of a specific translation. The ability to harness and exploit the wealth of information available on the Web is an indispensable part of modern translational competence. The disposable corpus is thus a truly professional construct, reflecting the need for on-demand resources for specific translation jobs, and as such has clear ties with the growing interest in translation memory CAT tools. However, Varantola underlines that assembling a corpus *ad hoc* does not mean assembling it haphazardly: criteria that have been around for a long time (cf. e.g. Atkins et al. 1992) can be adapted to the specific needs of (future) translators, and to the resources at their disposal. Every effort should be made to train learners to be discriminating in their choice of corpus texts.

Belinda Maia is also concerned with the creation of disposable *ad hoc* corpora, this time both comparable and parallel, with an emphasis on terminology extraction. She describes experiences with undergraduates and postgraduates in Portugal, confronting problematic questions such as the sector-specific competence required, and the availability and reliability of texts on the Web (one of the principal obstacles she encountered was the limited number of available texts in Portuguese compared with 'major' languages such as English and French). She argues that corpus construction and terminology extraction should be integral parts of a translator education curriculum. Tony McEnery and Paul Baker also stress the need for corpus research and development in minor European languages, but in addition underline the importance of collecting samples of native language use in non-native contexts, such as Asian languages spoken/ written in the UK. An unusual corpus type, one might think, yet one that corresponds to the current needs of professional linguists and NLP experts. The major corpus construction projects in Europe have focused exclusively on indigenous European languages, yet these languages are seldom the main target in domestic translation markets. It is not difficult to envisage other areas of research where this kind of 'minority corpus' could prove invaluable (sociolinguistic studies of intercultural communication being but the first to come to mind).

A very different approach is taken by Malmkjær, who illustrates the potential of a combination of single-author corpora and *star* corpora (made up of one original and many translations) in illuminating particular issues regarding writer and translator behaviour. Her claim that "there are real-life translation problems which corpora cannot help us with if we stick to the standard methods and the standard corpora" derives from her rejection of the assumption that past linguistic behaviour is a model for future behaviour. To show the need for specialized translational corpora to solve specialized problems (rather than relying on "mighty standard corpora"), she examines a number of translations of the Hans Christian Andersen tale *The Princess on the Pea*, as well as other works by the same writer in the fairy-tale genre. She then illustrates the power of the "rogue translation", the moment of creative inspiration rather than reliance on past performance, with a passage from Barbara Haveland's translation of Peter Høeg's *Forestilling om det tyvende århundrede* (*The History of Danish Dreams*).

The need to explore uses which might seem unorthodox in relation to standard corpus practice would, we believe, be agreed on by most of the contributors to this volume. Certainly it goes well with Johansson's discussion of *stars and diamonds*, which presents a series of complex corpus models, with particular reference to recent work at the University of Oslo. He gives an idea of the range of investigations that might be undertaken today with the help of corpora, envisaging an exciting array of new directions and horizons for research.

As he notes, a tendency towards diversity in corpus typologies is observable in corpus linguistics as a whole. Yet what these papers also suggest, taken together, is the will and need of theorists and practitioners in translation-related fields to recast input from different sources in terms of their needs and priorities, developing tools and resources specifically for translation purposes (be they descriptive, theoretical, or applied), rather than adapting those developed with other priorities in mind (e.g. monolingual and contrastive descriptive linguistics, or language pedagogy).

## 3.2 Customisable corpora, flexible users

We are using the term 'translator education' rather than 'translator training' to underline our belief that corpus work should help future translators increase their autonomy and flexibility, and that such experience should prove educationally valuable as well as professionally advantageous. By *flexibility* we mean the importance of adapting tools and strategies to specific pedagogic or research priorities. There are two aspects to flexibility: one is the provision of tools (corpora and interrogation software) that allow for it, while the other is users' ability to bend such tools to their concerns – a matter of awareness that becomes all the more important when learners interact with corpora without the mediation of teachers or material writers.

The requirement for tools to be flexible is voiced by Bowker and Bennison, who describe possible groupings within their Student Translation Archive (e.g. all translations of the same source text, all translations belonging to the same subject field, translations of source texts from the same subject fields but different source languages, etc.), illustrating how the associated software allows other sub-corpora to be created, depending on the user's priorities. They outline the merits and drawbacks of the archive and the interrogation software, still both in the experimental stage, as well as plans for future development.

Varantola's disposable corpora may also be viewed as quintessentially 'flexible': the corpus to be sampled is a virtual one, a subset of web texts, that comes into existence as the need arises, to be discarded on completion of the task. The adaptability of a corpus created 'on the fly' is however gained at the expense of such traditional design concerns as representativeness and balance. The importance of adaptability is also emphasized

by Frankenberg-Garcia and Santos: *Compara*, the Portuguese-English
Parallel (bidirectional) Corpus, modelled on the English-Norwegian Parallel Corpus, is (a) open-ended, so as to remain as close as possible to the
(future) concerns of users and thus develop in accordance with their needs,
and (b) modular, allowing users to search, for example, only texts belonging to one geographic variety of English and/or Portuguese, only texts
written before/after a certain date, only texts by one particular author/
translator or group of authors/translators, or to pick and choose among
the texts available (for example by genre), thus assembling truly 'user-
defined', tailor-made sub-corpora. As the authors note, "the responsibility
of achieving balance [...] and of judging the representativeness of the
corpus for any given study is left in the hands of the user".

This leads us on to our second point: the flexibility of users (rather
than of tools), here viewed as an ability to develop strategies for corpus
use which take full advantage of their potential in relation to the priorities and constraints of the pedagogic, learning, research, or professional
framework in which those users are operating. Flexibility in this sense is
a consequence of awareness (realising that there is a problem and for-
mulating appropriate questions), resourcefulness (knowing where to
look for solutions to a problem, and how to assemble resources), and
reflectiveness (being able to interpret results, draw conclusions, etc.:
Bernardini 2000).

Whilst any approach to a didactic use of corpora is bound to take cor-
pus-user interaction into account, this becomes of crucial significance when
learners are not simply presented with evidence, but are expected to browse
corpora for themselves, without the mediation of a teacher who 'digests'
data and offers generalisations. Natalie Kübler describes an experiment
aiming to enhance learners' awareness of the value of various computer-
ized resources, including existing monolingual corpora (both general and
specialized), parallel corpora, SYSTRAN and the Web, as well as their
ability to exploit these resources successfully. She argues that learning to
use corpora and interrogation software can provide future translators with
technical skills which, although not traditionally associated with translation, are becoming increasingly necessary for language professionals.

An emphasis on the resourcefulness and flexibility of users is one of
the basic tenets of data-driven language learning (Johns 1991). Learner
(and teacher) awareness relating to strategies of corpus construction and
analysis appears even more central in translator education. As mentioned
above, in her paper Malmkjær criticises the prescriptiveness inherent in

much corpus use in the field of translation, pleading for an approach in which the authority of the corpus is less absolute. Creativity and inventiveness on the part of future translators needs to be encouraged, even where this might seem to break an established 'norm' (see also Kenny 2001 on strategies and creativity in translation). Pearson's discussion of parallel corpus use for determining "what strategies professional translators employ to solve different translation problems" does not contradict Malmkjær's point. Pearson suggests that "there may be many different answers to what might appear to some to be a simple question", and that parallel corpora may provide a wider inventory of possibilities than a single translator is likely to come up with. By way of illustration she discusses a small parallel corpus of popular science articles from *Scientific American* and their translations into French in *Pour la Science*. She concentrates on renderings of culture-specific information, particularly names of people and institutions, in order to establish whether the corpus can be of assistance to students in drawing up their own translation guidelines. What emerges from her account is that choosing the most appropriate solution from the many in the corpus is far from trivial, requiring significant decision-making capacities (as also underlined in Varantola's paper).

Using corpora can provide opportunities to engage, and hence develop, such capacities, particularly where no clear solution to the problem is available. Similarly, the experience of constructing corpora, even inadequate ones, can offer the learner a bottom-up perspective on the texts that make up the corpus, and highlight the methodological limits of the corpus as tool, as well as its potential (Aston 1999). In other words, and however paradoxically, corpora can and should be employed to *problematise* rather than simplify the task of (future) translators. The greatest pedagogic value of the instrument lies, we suggest, in its *thought-provoking*, rather than *question-answering*, potential.

## 4. Conclusion: Good corpora and good corpus users

Summing up, the papers in this volume discuss various ways of building and using appropriate corpora for translation purposes. But as a corpus is only as good as its use(r)s, they also discuss ways of guiding learners to become better corpus builders and users. We believe, with Malmkjær, that used unreflectively, corpora may be dangerous, and that "sometimes it is better to break a norm rather than obey it, the trick is knowing when".

Even the most specific, most carefully-constructed, most flexible corpora will rarely provide straightforward answers to the translator's questions. But then very little is straightforward in language use, and translation is no exception. Corpus resources and software tools are at most useful tricks in the translator's bag. How best to teach and learn to 'know when' is a matter for translator education to determine, theoretically and empirically. The papers in this volume highlight both these aspects of corpus use in the classroom, describing first-hand experiences of corpus development and use for translation teaching, and providing, we hope, a source of inspiration for other researchers and practitioners in the field.

## Acknowledegment

Our sincerest thanks go to Guy Aston, in the first place for his support and assistance, especially in the revision stage, but most of all for coming up with a mean idea for a couple of conferences. Here's to many more...

# References

Aston, Guy (1999) 'Corpus Use and Learning to Translate', in Susan Bassnett, Rosa Maria Bollettieri Bosinelli and Margherita Ulrych (eds) *Translation Studies Revisited, Textus,* 12 (2), Genova: Tilgher, 289-314.

------ (2000) 'I corpora come risorse per la traduzione e per l'apprendimento', in Silvia Bernardini and Federico Zanettin (eds) *I corpora nella didattica della traduzione,* Bologna: CLUEB, 21-30.

Atkins, Sue, Jeremy Clear and Nicholas Ostler (1992) 'Corpus Design Criteria', *Literary and Linguistic Computing* 7: 1-16.

Baker, Mona (1993) 'Corpus Linguistics and Translation Studies – Implications and Applications', in Mona Baker, Gill Francis and Elena Tognini-Bonelli (eds) *Text and Technology. In Honour of John Sinclair,* Philadelphia and Amsterdam: John Benjamins, 233-252.

Bernardini, Silvia (2000) *Competence, Capacity, Corpora. A Study in Corpus-Aided Language Learning,* Bologna: CLUEB.

------ and Federico Zanettin (eds) (2000) *I Corpora nella Didattica della Traduzione – Corpus Use and Learning to Translate,* Bologna: CLUEB.

Caminade, Monique and Anthony Pym (1995) *Les Formations en Traduction et Inter-prétation. Essai de Recensement Mondial,* Paris: Société Française des Traducteurs.

Granger, Sylviane (ed) (1998) *Learner English on Computer,* Harlow: Longman.

Holmes, James (1988) *Translated! Papers on Literary Translation and Trans-*

*lation Studies*, Amsterdam: Rodopi.

Johns, Tim (1991) 'Should You Be Persuaded: Two Examples of Data Driven Learning', in Tim Johns and Philip King (eds) *Classroom Concordancing, ELR Journal*, 4 (special issue), 1-16.

------ (1997) 'Reciprocal DDL Materials', *Virtual DDL Library*, online: http://web.bham.ac.uk/johnstf/ddl_lib.htm#reciproc

Kenny, Dorothy (2001) *Lexis and Creativity in Translation*, Manchester: St Jerome.

Kiraly, Don (2000) *A Social Constructivist Approach to Translator Education*, Manchester: St Jerome.

Laviosa, Sara (1997) 'How Comparable Can 'Comparable Corpora' Be?', *Target* 9:2, 289-319.

Olohan, Maeve and Mona Baker (2000) 'Reporting *that* in Translated English: Evidence for Subconscious Processes of Explicitation?', *Across Languages and Cultures* 1(2): 141-158.

Øverås, Linn (1998) 'In Search of the Third Code: An Investigation of Norms in Literary Translation', *Meta* 43(4): 571-588.

Pearson, Jennifer (1998) *Terms in Context*, Amsterdam and Philadelphia: John Benjamins.

Seidlhofer, Barbara (2000) 'Operationalizing Intertextuality: Using Learner Corpora for Learning', in Lou Burnard and Tony McEnery (eds) *Rethinking Language Pedagogy from a Corpus Perspective*, Frankfurt am Main: Peter Lang, 207-223.

Sinclair, John (1991) *Corpus, Concordance, Collocation*, Oxford: Oxford University Press.

------ (1996) *EAGLES Preliminary Recommendations on Corpus Typology*, online: http://www.ilc.pi.cnr.it/EAGLES96/corpustyp/corpustyp.html

Somers, Harold (1998) 'Machine Translation', in Mona Baker (ed) *Routledge Encyclopedia of Translation Studies*, London and New York: Routledge, 140-148.

Svartvik, Jan (1992) 'Corpus Linguistics Comes of Age', in Jan Svartvik (ed) *Directions in Corpus Linguistics. Proceedings of Nobel Symposium 82, Stockholm, 4-8 August 1991*, Berlin: Mouton de Gruyter, 7-13.

Toury, Gideon (1995) *Descriptive Translation Studies and Beyond*, Amsterdam and Philadelphia: John Benjamins.

Véronis, Jean (ed) (2000) *Parallel Text Processing*, Amsterdam: Kluwer.

# Using Parallel Texts in the Translator Training Environment

JENNIFER PEARSON

*This paper aims to examine whether and how parallel corpora can be used to inform specialized translation courses. Comparable corpora have already found their niche in translator training, and we will argue that parallel corpora can be used as a complement to comparable corpora because there will be times when comparable corpora will not suffice. A small parallel collection of popular science articles translated from English into French will be used to illustrate the point, and we will look at how translation students might use resources of this type to help them in translation.*

## 1.  Introduction

This paper examines whether and how parallel corpora can be used to inform specialized translation courses. Comparable corpora are already being used quite extensively in the translator training environment in order to assist students with making appropriate lexical and phraseological choices (Pearson 1996; Zanettin 1998; Bowker 1998); the underlying premise is that comparable corpora are a richer resource for this type of information than conventional resources such as dictionaries. Parallel corpora, on the other hand, have not yet found their place in the translator training environment. While they are being used increasingly in translation research and are also used frequently to teach *language*, there is little written evidence to suggest that they are being used to teach *translation*.

It is our belief that parallel corpora have a role to play in the translator training environment, that students can use parallel corpora to help them with translation and that the findings from corpus-based studies of parallel corpora can, and should, inform the design and implementation of specialized translation courses. This would help us to realize Baker's contention that one of the objectives of a corpus-based approach to the study of parallel texts should be "to establish objectively how translators overcome difficulties of translation in practice, and to use this evidence to provide realistic models for trainee translators" (Baker, 1995: 231).

In the first section of this paper, we will outline why we believe parallel corpora and comparable corpora have complementary roles to play in the translator training environment. We will then describe the collection of texts that we used for our investigation and highlight some features of this collection that we believe to be of particular interest to us. In the main body of the paper, we will examine how translation students might use a resource such as this as an aid to translation. We aim to demonstrate that there are some translation problems that can only be resolved by examining parallel corpora.

## 2.   Comparable vs. parallel corpora

Comparable corpora, i.e. collections of texts in two or more languages containing texts of the same type and dealing with the same domain, are an invaluable resource for translation teachers and students. Students tend to use them in much the same way as they would a dictionary, i.e. to check for correct terminology, to identify appropriate collocates. They use comparable corpora to discover typical ways of saying things in a particular language in a particular text type in a particular subject field. Thus, they might discover that certain syntactic structures are more prevalent in one language than another, that the use of certain sets of words (e.g. adjectives and adverbs) differs from one language to another. Teachers will use comparable corpora in much the same way as students when preparing their translation classes, and they may also use comparable corpora as an aid to evaluating students' work (cf. Bowker 1999; Pearson 1999). In fact, it is here that comparable corpora really come into their own because translation teachers sometimes have difficulty explaining to students why they believe a particular translation choice to be *unnatural* and therefore inappropriate. Access to comparable corpora allows teachers to a) validate their own intuitions, and b) use the corpus evidence as a basis for their explanation to students. Students tend to be much more receptive to corrections that are supported by hard evidence.

It is clear that the reasons for using comparable corpora in the translator training environment are not in dispute here. What we would suggest, however, is that comparable corpora will not suffice in all cases. This is because the texts in a comparable corpus are produced in a different context from those in a parallel corpus. Generally speaking, texts in comparable corpora are originals, i.e. they have not been translated from another language. They provide evidence of language behaving naturally in a *monolingual* environment. Parallel corpora, on the other hand, contain texts and their translations. Thus, they contain evidence not only of language produced in a *monolingual* environment (the source texts) but also of language produced in a *bi-* or *multilingual* environment (the translations). There is evidence to suggest that the language used in translation may differ from the language used in the production of an original source text (Laviosa 1998). Thus, investigations of parallel corpora may allow students to see how writers, i.e. translators, behave when constrained by the existence of a text composed in another language. Translators have to act as cultural and linguistic mediators, negotiating their way between languages and between cultures. They have to gauge how much of the material in a source text is directly transferable to the target language, how much of it needs to be adapted or localized in some way, whether any of it can, or indeed should, be omitted. The answers to questions of this nature cannot be found in comparable corpora because these issues never arise in a monolingual text-producing environment. They only arise because of the constraints of a text composed in another language. The answers must therefore be sought in parallel corpora. By studying parallel corpora, particularly aligned parallel corpora, translation students have the opportunity to see for themselves what strategies professional translators employ to solve different translation problems. They can learn how information is conveyed, whether any information is lost, adapted or misrepresented in the process. By observing what has happened, they can begin to devise their own translation strategies.

## 3. The collection of texts

In the remaining sections of this paper, we propose to look at a small collection of texts to illustrate how translation students might use a parallel corpus as an aid to translation. The subject of investigation is a collection of articles from *Scientific American* and their French translations published in *Pour la Science*, as well as a collection of articles published in *Pour la Science* written originally in French. The texts were collected in a number of ways: via e-mail from the publishers of *Pour la Science,* downloaded from the *Scientific American* website and scanned using OCR software. The text collection process was quite time consuming, and proofreading and editing proved to be much more tedious than envisaged. Once all texts had been proofread and edited, they were prepared for linguistic analysis. *Minmark*, developed by David Woolls in Birmingham, U.K. was used for this purpose; it provides minimal mark-up of texts (i.e. it marks up sentence and paragraph breaks) to facilitate the production of bilingual concordances. Once the texts have been marked up, *MultiConcord* (another tool developed by David Woolls (1996)) is used to produce bilingual concordances.

| Publication | Tokens | Types | TT ratio | Std TT ratio | No. of sentences | Sentence length | Std. Sentence length |
|---|---|---|---|---|---|---|---|
| SA | 187,159 | 15,613 | 8.34 | 45.27 | 6,737 | 27.60 | 16.07 |
| PLStr | 168,518 | 17,478 | 10.37 | 44.10 | 4,899 | 34.05 | 20.78 |
| PLSfr | 136,908 | 16,123 | 11.78 | 44.36 | 4,476 | 29.02 | 22.79 |

**Table 1:** Statistics for 63 articles from *Scientific American* and their translations in *Pour la Science* and 45 articles in the control collection

As table 1 shows, the collection of texts is relatively small, with only 187,159 tokens in the source texts and 168,518 tokens in the target texts. Readers may note that the number of sentences in the translations is significantly lower than in the source texts. This is because sizeable segments in the source texts have been omitted from the translations. There are many possible reasons for this which, because of space constraints, we do not propose to discuss here. Suffice it to say that there is considerable evidence of localization and adaptation during the translation process, i.e. adjusting the text to meet the expectations and needs of the target audience. We will see some examples of this in our later discussion of the translation of culture-specific references.

## 4.  Using a parallel corpus to resolve translation problems

As already mentioned, translation students can use parallel corpora to see how professional translators have overcome specific translation problems. Here, we look to our parallel collection to see how a certain number of phenomena have been handled. It should be said at the outset that the discussion which follows is mainly illustrative. It is designed to show the potential usefulness of a parallel corpus; it is clear that with such a small collection as the one used here, any conclusions that are drawn must be deemed to be tentative.

# 5. Investigating the translation of culture-specific information

In my experience as a teacher of translation, and in my own experience as a professional translator, there is one question that arises again and again, namely what to do with culture-specific information. Culture-specific information is information about statistics, events, institutions, organizations, individuals in the source culture. Should such references be translated? In their entirety? Should explanations be provided for the target audience? If so, in what form? Should references that are deemed to be too local to be of relevance to the target audience simply be omitted? Should they be replaced by equivalent information in the target culture? How can a translator begin to decide what is the appropriate solution? If we look to our parallel collection of texts we find that varying solutions have been adopted. Let us look at one or two examples.

The source texts in the collection frequently contain references to individual researchers, their work and the institutions or universities to which they are affiliated. When we look to the target texts to see how these references have been rendered in translation, we find that the names of the individual researchers are often omitted, as the following example demonstrates. Here two apparently eminent individuals are named and their affiliations are specified in the source text; in the target texts they are simply referred to as *les psychiatres*.

> Alexander Leighton, now professor emeritus of social psychiatry
> at the Harvard School of Public Health, T. A. Lambo, formerly
> deputy director general of WHO

We are not suggesting that this is what students should do; we know that there is no easy answer to the question of what to do with culture specific references. We believe, however, that by looking at how professional translators have solved these problems, student translators can at least obtain some indication of what to do.

Some of the source texts contain quite a lot of statistical information. What is one to do in this situation? Should the information relating to the source culture be replaced by equivalent information relating to the target culture, as has been done in the following example from the collection?

> In the U.S. alone, AIDS has killed more than 350,000 people and
> has become the principal cause of death among those 24 to 44

years old.

En France, le sida a déjà tué plus de 50 000 personnes, et il est
devenu une des principales causes de mortalité chez les personnes
âgées de 24 à 44 ans.

Here again, as all professional translators know, there is no straightforward answer to the question of what to do with this type of information
because the answer will usually depend on a number of factors (for example, the publisher's guidelines, the nature of the target audience, the aim
of the article). What is important here, however, is that students can again
see for themselves what actually happens in translation and can appreci-
ate that different solutions may be appropriate for different situations.

Let us now look at the treatment of one other type of culture-specific
reference in our collection, namely the names of institutions and universities. Let us start with the names of universities. 102 universities are named
in the collection. In 66 instances, the name of the university was translated using the term *université*; in 36 instances, the name of the university
was either translated by other means or was not translated at all.

If we look at those instances where the name of the university was not
translated at all, we find that in seven instances, the entire paragraph containing the reference to the named university has been omitted from the
translation. The omitted paragraphs generally contain more detailed information about some topic already introduced in the preceding paragraph.
Thus, additional information about a survey carried out at the University
of Alaska is omitted, as is additional information about pain and distress
caused to animals during drug testing, additional information relating to
research on bacterial pore-forming proteins, additional information regarding the lack of ethical introspection in relation to animal testing, etc.
We do not plan to dwell any further here on these instances as we believe
that these instances of failure to translate are part of a larger question
(namely, when is it appropriate to omit an entire paragraph or paragraphs
from a translation?) and do not really help us with our search for appropriate translation strategies.

Let us look instead at instances where the name of the university is not
translated and where the reasons for not doing so may be different. In our
collection of texts, universities named in the source text but not translated
include the University of Adelaide in Australia, the University of Ala-
bama at Birmingham, the University of Texas at Austin, the University of
Cape Town, the University of Arizona, the University of Darmstadt, the
University of Houston, the University of Illinois, the University of Iowa,

the University of Notre Dame, the University of Miami, the University of Texas-Houston. In the instances involving the above named universities, the entire sentence in which the name of the university appeared in the source text was not translated. Furthermore, no explicit reference to the university or to people associated with the university was made in subsequent or earlier sentences in the paragraph. We believe that it is possible that the references to these universities may have been omitted from the translations because the translators may have thought that a) the information was not crucial for the target audience or b) the researchers named did not have a sufficiently large international reputation to warrant inclusion in the target text. Clearly, a student translator would not be in a position to make decisions of this nature, and most professional translators would also be reluctant to make such alterations to a scientific text without the prior authorization and approval of the publisher. It is nonetheless interesting to see how the same type of culture-specific reference can be treated in a number of different ways.

If we look now to the names of universities that have indeed been translated but not literally, we find that *the University of California at Berkeley* is translated as *l'Université de Berkeley, the University of California at San Francisco* as *l'Université de San Francisco, the University of California at San Diego* as *l'Université de San Diego, the University of California at Los Angeles* as *l'Université de Los Angeles.* Similarly, *State University of New York at Stony Brook* is translated as *l'Université de Stony Brook, State University of New York at Albany* is translated as *l'Université d'Albany.* The emphasis appears to be more on the place where the university is located than on the name of the university itself. What one might conclude from these and many other similar examples in the corpus is that the translator believes the reader is more likely to be acquainted with the name of the place where the university is located. This practice is analogous to English speakers referring to the Sorbonne University in Paris as *the Sorbonne* rather than as *Paris I.*

Let us now look at one last set of translation solutions for the names of universities. When a source text contains a reference to a university in Europe, the country in which the university is located is often named as well in the source text. Thus, readers will find reference to the *University of Lund in Sweden, University of Mainz in Germany, University of Louvain Medical School in Belgium* in the source texts. There are also instances where the country is not named; this is the case for example with references to the University of Oxford and the University of Geneva. The authors of the source texts appear to be making judgements about their readers' knowledge of European geography; alternatively they may be making judgements about the reputations of the universities. Thus, the authors may think it appropriate to specify that Lund is in Sweden, Mainz in Germany etc. because they are not sure that their (American) English-speaking audience already know this or that they will have heard of these universities previously. In the translations, we find, perhaps not surprisingly, that the name of the country has been omitted, and that the names of the above universities are translated simply as *l'Université de Lund, l'Université de Mayence, l'Université Catholique de Louvain.* Like the writers of the source texts, the translators appear to have made judgements about their (European) French-speaking readers' knowledge of the geography of Europe. They assume that their readers will know Europe sufficiently well to know in which country these universities are located. For instances of this type, it would be relatively easy for a translation student to devise a translation rule or guideline which would enable them to justify the omission of geographical information when it is perceived to be redundant for the target audience.

We also investigated the treatment of the names of institutes in translation. 32 institutes were named in the source texts, the names of 20 of these were translated directly; in 10 instances, they were not translated at all and they were translated by other means in the two remaining instances.

If we look at the instances where the name of the Institute is not translated, there is just one instance where the entire paragraph in which the sentence appears in the source text is missing from the translation. In the remaining nine instances, one could argue that, as with the university names which were not translated, the translators made a decision about the importance either of the named institutes themselves or of naming them in this particular context. The institutes whose names are not translated are the following: *the California Institute of Technology, the National Institute of Standards and Technology, the Paul Ehrlich Institute in Langen, Germany, the National Institute of Public Health and the Environment in the Netherlands, the National Institute of Mental Health, the Babraham Institute in Cambridge, England.* In those instances where the names of the institutes were translated, the translations were not always literal. Thus, *the Burnham Institute in La Jolla, California* is translated as *l'Institut Burnham, en Californie.* In this instance, the translator probably felt that the reader did not need to know the exact location in California. In other instances, we find the phrase *National Institute* being translated as *Institut américain*. Thus, *the National Institute of Standards and Technology* is translated as *l'Institut américain de normalisation*, *the National Cancer Institute (NCI)* as *l'Institut américain du cancer*, *the National Institute of Allergy and Infectious Diseases* as *l'Institut américain des maladies allergiques et infectieuses*. Here, the translators have opted to translate *national* by *américain* rather than *national*, probably in an attempt to avoid ambiguity in the target text. This is an interesting solution and one that might not immediately suggest itself to a student translator who might be more likely to translate *National Institute* as *l'institut national... aux Etats-Unis*.

## 6. Concluding remarks

In this paper we set out to demonstrate that parallel corpora have a role to play in the translator training environment, a role that is quite different from the one played by comparable corpora. We wanted to show that parallel corpora can provide students with evidence of how "translators overcome difficulties of translation in practice" (Baker 1995: 231). We chose to look at how a very small set of culture specific references were translated in order to try and establish whether the corpus evidence could help students to draw up their own translation guidelines. We chose to focus on culture specific references because these are notoriously difficult for trainee translators and also, we would argue, for translation teachers. As we were working with a rather small collection of texts drawn from a single source, we were aware that any conclusions that we drew would have to be treated as tentative. Our main objective was to demonstrate that parallel corpora could be useful. It is clear from the cases discussed here that we did not have enough occurrences in our collection to allow us to infer rules for the treatment of culture-specific references. Our investigation did, however, allow us to demonstrate that there may be many different answers to what might appear to some to be a simple question, and that study of a parallel corpus might reveal solutions that had not been imagined. Parallel corpora are thus confirmed to have an important role to play in the translator training environment.

# References

Baker, Mona (1995) 'Corpora in Translation Studies: An Overview and Some Suggestions for Future Research', *Target* 7(2): 223-243.

Bowker, Lynne (1998) 'Using Specialized Monolingual Native-Language Corpora as a Translation Resource: A Pilot Study', *Meta* 43(4): 631-651.

------ (1999) 'Using a Corpus to Assess Student Translations: A Pilot Study', in Barbara Lewandowska-Tomaszczyk and Patrick James Melia (eds), *PALC '99: Practical Applications in Language Corpora,* Frankfurt am Main: Peter Lang, 529-540.

Laviosa, Sara (1998) 'The English Comparable Corpus: A Resource and a Methodology', in Lynne Bowker, Michael Cronin, Dorothy Kenny and Jennifer Pearson (eds) *Unity in Diversity? Current Trends in Translation Studies,* Manchester: St. Jerome, 101-112.

Pearson, Jennifer (1996) 'Electronic Texts and Concordances in the Translation Classroom', *Teanga* 16: 86-96.

------ (1999) 'Using Specialized Comparable Corpora to Evaluate Student Translations' in Barbara Lewandowska-Tomaszczyk and Patrick James Melia (eds) *PALC '99: Practical Applications in Language Corpora,* Frankfurt am Main: Peter Lang, 541-552.

Woolls, David (1996) *MultiConcord.* http://www.copycatch.freeserve.co.uk

Zanettin, Federico (1998) 'Bilingual Comparable Corpora and the Training of Translators', *Meta* 43(4): 616-630.

# Corpora and LSP Translation

NATALIE KÜBLER

*This paper reports an experimental approach in the training of LSP trans-lators by introducing digital corpora and corpus manipulation tools. The use of corpora in LSP translation is nothing new. In specialized transla-tion, translators also work as terminologists, as they have to make up a list of the terms of a specific domain, as well as the list of their transla-tions into the target language. People working in terminology have been using paper corpora for a long time to look for term candidates and their phraseology. The great change in the past few years stems from the greater accessibility of digitized corpora and powerful personal computers. This paper shows how the use of corpora and corpus query tools can greatly improve and facilitate the work of translators.*

## 1. Introduction

This paper discusses an experimental approach to the training of special-ized translators through the application of corpus query tools to textual data. The use of corpora within the frame of translation and languages for special purposes (LSPs) is nothing really new. In specialized translation, translators often have to work as terminologists, as they have to deal with terms (and their translation into the target language) that are specific to a subject area that they may not know very well. People working in termi-nology have been using paper corpora for a long time, to search for term candidates and their phraseology. The great developments in recent years have been the result of a greater accessibility to electronic corpora and powerful personal computers.

The experiment took place at the *Department of Intercultural Studies and Applied Languages* ("*Etudes interculturelles et langues appliquées*") at the University Paris 7. The students involved in the experiment were undergraduates and postgraduates preparing for a diploma in specialized translation and language engineering. The approach I used took the form of projects based on group work.

The first section of this paper describes the pedagogic objectives of this experiment, as well as the students taking part. Section 2 describes the corpora and the tools used. The projects run during the academic year are described in Section 3, while the use of corpora and the results obtained are detailed in Sections 4 and 5.

# 2.   Students groups and pedagogic objectives

The students were divided into two groups: undergraduates and postgraduates. Since postgraduate students have more experience than undergraduate students, the pedagogic objectives were slightly different.

## 2.1  Students and student subjects

Undergraduate students are in their fourth year of university study (the French degree called 'Maîtrise'). At this stage they do not usually have any professional experience as translators. They are trained, as full-time students, to translate from English into French, and from German or Spanish into French. The vast majority of them have been taught basic computer skills for the humanities, i.e. word processing, spreadsheet software, database use and Web browsing. Most of them have a basic knowledge of general linguistics, but know nothing about Natural Language Processing (NLP) or Corpus Linguistics.

Postgraduate students are in their fifth year of study (the French degree 'DESS', a postgraduate professional degree that leads to work with private companies and not to a PhD). Postgraduate students are divided into two groups:

- IL: 'Industrie des Langues' (Language Industry);
- TS: 'Traduction Spécialisée' (Specialized Translation).

The first one (IL) is more oriented towards the language industry; students are taught more computing skills, such as working with Unix, and using SGML/XML, HTML, SQL, PHP, and perl. SGML/XML and HTML are markup languages, the former being an international standard to format documents, the latter being the most widely-used format to build Web-pages. SQL is a language used to query databases and PHP is used to build databases on the Web. Perl is a programming language that is widely used to process natural language. There is increasing demand, from companies dealing with NLP, translation, localisation etc., for multilingual linguists or translators with skills in computer techniques and programming languages. Students are trained to translate mostly from English into French.

The second group (TS) usually translates from English into French, and either German, Spanish or Portuguese into French. As some of them are not native speakers of French, other translation pairs are also accepted (e.g. English into German or Greek into English). The TS group learns fewer computing skills, i.e. basic skills in HTML and nothing about Unix. The two postgraduate groups work part-time in private companies, i.e., they spend one week at university, and the other one with a company, as interns. They have to carry out various tasks depending on the company they work with: translating technical documents, post-editing, technical writing, building term bases, building electronic dictionaries for Natural Language Processing systems, and manipulating texts using different tools.

## 2.2 Pedagogic objectives

There are two types of pedagogic objective in the experimental approach described: the general objectives are the same for the undergraduate and postgraduate students; the particular objectives depend on the knowledge and situation specific to undergraduate or postgraduate studies, which are detailed below. These differences also meant different projects.

### 2.2.1 General objectives
The students concerned are generally computer-literate at both undergraduate and postgraduate level. As students in specialized translation, they have to build term bases in varied areas:

- health-related subjects;
- cats fur;
- wine-making;
- computer science;
- astronomy;
- geology;
- arachnology.

Students are used to working on paper corpora and extracting potential terms manually. The general objectives of the experiment consisted in graduating from paper to electronic corpora: the aim was to help students become familiar with electronic corpora and corpus query tools, and to use the Web as a 'mega-corpus',[1] browsing it for linguistic (and encyclopaedic) information, as underlined by Maia (e.g. 2000). Linking the paper corpora which students have to collect in their terminology projects with electronic corpora and the Web resulted also in the gathering of corpora in the various subject areas students were working on. Another general objective was to help people learn to work in groups on specific projects in order to prepare them for the non-academic world, in which deadlines must be met for job completion.

### 2.2.2  *Particular objectives for undergraduate students*
The full-time students in their fourth year at university have never translated a whole document (there is no translation project proper until the fourth year). As they have always translated text samples, they only have a vague idea of the processes involved in the translation of a document outside the university. Our aim was to show them the tasks that must be carried out in the 'real' world and the steps that must be taken beyond the process of translating itself, such as documentation, terminology, working with experts, proofreading etc.

### 2.2.3  *Particular objectives for postgraduate students*
The postgraduate students already know of the processes associated with translation. However, they are still quite wary of computers, especially machine translation (MT) systems. The pedagogic objective here lies in convincing students, especially the TS group, that MT systems can be useful tools (and are no threat) for human translators. They therefore learn how to use a Web-based MT system (Systran) as a tool to help them in the translation process. A beneficial side-effect is that they are shown how corpora can help enhance MT systems, which is a bonus, as some of our students work in NLP companies.

## 3.   Corpora and Tools

The corpora used are accessible on a Web site via tools which were developed at the University of Paris 13 (Foucou and Kübler 2000) and have

---

[1] The Web can help find linguistic information, but is of course not as balanced and reliable as a carefully chosen collection of texts.
[2] http://wall.jussieu.fr

migrated to the University Paris 7. They can be accessed at the DESS Web site. [2]

## 3.1 Corpora

The corpora accessible to the students consist of monolingual, comparable, and parallel corpora in English and French. There are two types of corpora: specialized language corpora (specialized corpora) and general language corpora.

### 3.1.1 Specialized corpora

Specialized corpora are here defined as a collection of texts dealing with a particular subject area, and written by experts for a varied readership (experts to experts, experts to students, experts to laymen). For the time being, the specialized corpora available on-line[3] deal with computer science, digital cameras, gene therapy, and video editing. The underlying philosophy of our corpus-collecting principles is to take advantage of the existing resources that are accessible on the Web. For the projects described below, the specialized corpora used were the Computer Science and the Digital Camera corpora.

*Computer Science:* Our computer science corpus has been collected to teach computational English to French-speaking students in computer science (Foucou and Kübler 2000). The corpus must therefore be representative of the different genres computer science students are confronted with: OS manuals, Internet manuals, newsgroups, specialized dictionaries, computer science jargon. This corpus was also used by our postgraduate students in the project that will be described below. The available corpora in this domain are the following:

> the Free On-Line Dictionary Of Computing: 500,000 words,
> the Internet Request For Comments (RFCs): 8,5 million words,
> the Unix manual (man): 1,6 million words,
> articles from *Wired*: 100,000 words,
> mails from computer science newsgroups: 100,000 words,
> the Linux HOWTOs: 500,000 words. The HOWTOs have been aligned with their French translation and thus are considered as a translation corpus.

---

[3] Some of the corpora used are not available outside the university for confidentiality reasons relating to the companies we work with.

*Digital Cameras:* All the documentation used comes from around twenty Web sites either in French or in English, and from user manuals. They can be accessed separately, although not all are accessible outside the university, for copyright reasons. The size of this corpus is around 400,000 words.

### 3.1.2   'General' corpora

Our aim is not to collect a general corpus of English or French, nevertheless a 'general' comparable corpus of newspapers is available to check the degree of specialization of a term. It is clear that using the British National Corpus or The Bank of English will provide more information about general rather than sector-specific English, though it is quite convenient to have this type of corpus at hand. The available newspapers in French and English are the following:

> *The Times:* 3.5 million words,
> *The Herald Tribune*: 1.5 million words
> *Le Monde*: 1 million words

A whole year of each of those newspapers has been collected.

## 3.2  Tools[4]

The concordancer to which students have access is based on perl-like regular expressions and allows queries containing POS tags. Although the concordancer uses POS tags on plain text, the words are not disambiguated, thus following Sinclair's (Sinclair 1991) view of using corpora. This allows the user to begin with as wide a search as possible and to narrow it little by little looking carefully at the results.

A common word in the field of digital cameras in French is the term *exposition* (*exposure*). Instead of looking up only *exposition*, the first step consists in finding all the sequences including *expos* in French. The search string is the following: \w*expos\w*, which will retrieve occurrences such as those shown in the short concordance sample 1:

---

[4] All the examples in the 'Tools' section come from our digital cameras corpora in French and in English.

La synchro lente permet au film d être **exposé** à l éclairage ambiant
exemple quand le sujet est sous- **exposé** (voir le Guide Rapide).
Trop sombre, une photographie est sous- **exposée** . Trop claire,
d obturateur au-dessus de 1/8.000 pour **exposer** correctement. La
expliquez-vous que je n arrive jamais à **exposer** correctement un
fréquemment trop claires et apparaissent **surexposées** . Le mode de
400 ISO et un flash intégré assure une **exposition** correcte

**Concordance 1.** A sample of concordance lines retrieved by the
regular expression \w**expos*\w*

This search result is teeming with terms and linguistic information, such
as the adjectives *sous-exposé* and *surexposé*. The extracts *le sujet est sous-
exposé* and *exposer correctement un groupe de personnes* reveal a
specialized use of the verb *exposer* and its compounds. In general French,
the argument in the direct object position cannot be either animate or human with the specific meaning it has here.

The next two search strings describe French compound noun structures often used to coin new terms in LSPs:

&N/\w+ de &N/\w+
&N/\w+ &A/\w+

The first one defines a multi-word noun composed of a noun followed by
the preposition *de* ('of') and followed again by a noun, while the second
one comprises a multi-word noun composed of a noun and an adjective.
As there is no POS disambiguation, the first results of this kind of search
are a little too wide, as shown in concordance 2:

La grande majorité des **amateurs de photo** numérique pense que la résolution de l
200-1200), vérification et **analyse de l** image en temps réel sur écran couleur à
la focale utilisée, et donc l **angle de champ**, ainsi que les accessoires montés) **
d un contraste élevé et d un **angle de vision** latéral étendu, l appareil photo
bonne qualité en A4. Si l **augmentation de la** taille d image est un plus, la nouvelle
incluse qui raine dans la **base de l** appareil-photo dans l' ensemble (verrou
Effect d images Livré: **cable de connexion**, drivers Le MAVICA MVC-FD 51 Prix:

**Concordance 2.** A sample of concordance lines retrieved by the
regular expression &N/\w+ de &N/\w+

This problem is readily solved by defining the minimum number of characters a word must contain as: *&N/\w{3,} de &N/\w{4,}*. In this case, words such as *la*, which can be either a definite article or a noun (a key in music), are discarded, and many terms in the domain of photography can be found using this method (concordance 3):

```
la balance des blancs TTL*, et la compensation de tons **. * Le Ni

fournit des informations sur la composition de photographies, en

Le dessus du contrôleur sont les configurations de foyer, d inst

réglage automatique de distance et confirmation de charge du fla
```

**Concordance 3.** A sample of concordance lines retrieved by the regular expression &N/\w{3,} de &N/\w{4,}

A tokenizer using perl-like regular expressions is also available. It sorts single word unit frequencies, but also all the words containing specific sequences. The following sequence describes all the words ending with the suffix *ible: \w+ible*. It results in a list containing words such as *accessible*, *compatible*, *flexible*, *impossible* etc.

# 4.   Project description

Differences in background as well as pedagogic objectives meant that the undergraduate and postgraduate students had to undertake different projects.

## 4.1   Undergraduate project and procedure

The undergraduate project consisted in translating a Web Site on digital cameras, collecting and using comparable corpora in English and French in this specific subject area. General language corpora were also available in English and French, as they are useful to test the degree of specialization of a term. The Web had to  be used as a huge corpus when more linguistic or encyclopaedic information was needed. The Web site chosen consisted of a series of reviews on digital cameras. The class was divided into groups of three, each group being responsible for the translation of one review and one of the following tasks:

- Downloading their review in HTML and plain text format
- Collecting documentation from the Web, user manuals

- Checking the documentation with an expert
- Collecting French and English corpora on digital cameras
- Completing a term base with terms in the two languages
- Translating their review
- Proofreading
- Creating the French Web site

Each group was also responsible for coordinating one of the different tasks, and for making the information available to the whole group:

- The corpora groups were in charge of merging the corpora collected by the different groups, deleting the duplicates, checking for possible mistakes and submitting the completed corpora to the coordinator so that she could integrate them into a concordancer;
- The terminology group set up a term base under *Microsoft Access* that other groups added to; they also had to check for consistency;
- The documentation group collected and commented on the various glossaries found by the other groups, and took charge of copyright problems;
- Two groups were responsible for proofreading the translations;
- The last group was responsible for creating the French Web site, linking the files and checking the HTML tagging (it should be noted however that this task was done in a parallel class in which students were taught the basics of HTML).

Everybody had to do a little of everything and each group was responsible for one task on behalf of the whole class.

## 4.2 Postgraduate project and procedure

As the aim for the postgraduate students was different, the project consisted in translating a part of the *Free On-Line Dictionary of Computing (FOLDOC)*[5] into French using:

- an on-line MT system (*SYSTRAN*);
- comparable corpora in general, and computer science (CS) corpora

---

[5] http://www.foldoc.org

in English and French ;
- parallel corpora (also called translation corpora) in which the source text was in CS English and the target text in CS French;
- the Web as a corpus and source of linguistic information.

Working in small groups, students elected to translate several entries in the same subject area, such as programming languages, networks, games, e-mail, the Web, operating systems and so on. The first step was to carry out a rough translation using the *SYSTRAN* MT system. The next step consisted in analyzing *SYSTRAN*'s translation problems at all linguistic and non-linguistic levels: format, lexicon, terminology, lexicon-grammar, syntax, semantics, and pragmatics. They then had to correct the translations. Working in a parallel course on HTML, each group had to publish their project on the Web.

## 4.3   A short presentation of  SYSTRAN

The *SYSTRAN* machine translation system is based on a transformer architecture: texts are translated sentence by sentence and input sentences are transformed into output sentences with the simplest possible parse. There is no complete parsing, thus no complete representation, of the sentence. A package of lexical and grammatical translation rules transform the source sentence into a target sentence, re-ordering words and taking into account phenomena such as agreement. This system has the advantage of being quite robust, carrying out a translation in any case, even when sentences are not grammatically correct. Obviously, the drawback of this type of system lies in the results which are not completely reliable. Some translations are surprisingly good, others have nothing to do with the source text. All well-known and difficult to parse phenomena, such as conjunctions, disjunctions, long-distance dependencies, and global ambiguity pose problems. Simpler issues, such as the position of noun modifiers in French and in English, are not always well managed:

> EN.   The IETF is a **large, open international community** of network designers, operators, vendors and researchers whose purpose is to coordinate the operation, management and evolution of the Internet and to resolve **short- and mid-range protocol and architectural issues.**

> FR. L'IETF est une **grande, ouverte communauté internationale** des créateurs de réseau, des opérateurs, des constructeurs et des chercheurs dont le but est coordonner l'exécution, la gestion et l'évolution de l'Internet et de les résoudre **protocole sous peu et de mi-portée et issues architecturales**.

Apart from the difficulties related to syntactic analysis, issues such as anaphora resolution or those connected with pragmatics and world knowledge are not taken into account in this MT system. As will be shown below, issues raised by translating LSPs can be dealt with using various types of corpora.

# 5. Working with comparable corpora

The first part of this paper dealt with specific projects and tools used as background information, before explaining the role of corpora. Corpora sustain all the work done in the two projects. The following description of their use in the projects will reveal the experimental approach adopted.

## 5.1 Understanding terms

When reading a text to be translated, translators are liable to find terms they will not understand because they are too specialized. The first use of corpora, here, is to help translators find definitions of specific terms that cannot be found in specialized dictionaries or glossaries. Pearson's (1998) approach to finding terms can be adapted in this case. In the subject area of digital cameras, the term *white balance* denotes a concept that is obscure to non-experts. Following Pearson's method of looking for terms, it is possible to search for the sequence *called .{0,30} white balance*, which allows the user to look up *called* followed by 0 up to 20 characters, spaces, symbols, punctuation marks, etc., followed by *white balance* in lower or upper case. It retrieves the following definition:

> These little marvels can automatically balance the color of light electronically so that nothing comes out looking too hot or too cold. It's **called 'White Balance'** (WB, for short), which simply means the camera tries to keep white objects fairly white, so they don't take on extreme color casts.

Another definition can be found using similar methods:

> White balance: function that allows you to have natural colors by
> **adapting the whites** to the light.

The following useful remarks can be drawn from these two definitions:

> 'white balance' can be abbreviated ('WB');
> the adjective 'white' can be nominalized (see 'adapting the whites').

## 5.2  Linguistic information

Obtaining more linguistic information about this term entails finding concordances for the left- and right-hand side contexts of 'white balance',
'WB' and 'whites' (see concordance 4 for selected concordances):

```
(SHQ-TIFF, SHQ, HQ, SQ-HIGH, SQ) White Balance (Auto, sunlight, cloudy, tungsten,
Gray Card (18%) and use the camera in White Balance Hold mode. When ever you move from one
the menu, as well as adjusting ISO and White Balance settings. Some other items of note
rundown of everything you can change: White balance (Auto, manual, sunlight, incandescent,
continuous shooting with exposure and white balance adjusted for every shot,
capabilities, exposure compensation, white balance adjustments, stitch assist, in-camera
Only the more advanced features like white balance and continuous modes need the menuing
on this in a second) and more. The white balance controls have some cool features,
Condition under which Preset white balance data is reset changed With Ver. 1.2,
away. It actually did better in the white balance department than my CP950 usually does!
With moderate compression I found the white balance feature to be a little strange. Instead
now onto another nice feature - manual white balance. In addition to auto, and presets for
The only way I've found to get accurate white balance in this room is to use manual white
shutter, infinite focus, and daylight white balance. It even tells you to use a tripod -
see quite a few examples of the cloudy white balance mode.) And that's all the manual
```

**Concordance 4.** A sample of concordance lines for the string *white balance*

The sequence (white balance)|(WB)|(whites) sorted by the right-hand
side context gives a list of possible multi-word units, for example:

> white balance setting, white balance mode, white balance control,
> white balance compensation, white balance system, white balance
> feature, white balance department, white balance thing.

In this case, the method consists in first checking whether other terms can be followed by *setting, mode, control* etc. If this is the case, it leads to a new list of terms. Then possible uses of verbs such as *to set, to control, to compensate* must be looked up to define the verb structures in which the term can be an argument, and which argumental position it takes. Linguistic intuition tells us that *white balance department* and *white balance thing* are not terms, but just idioms that can be found in the general language. However, the non-native speaker of English, translating from English into French, can compare the use of <term> *department* and <term> *thing* in the general English corpus; the idiomatic structures *in the glamour department* or *in the speed department* are found and present the same use as *in the white balance department*. About the <term> *thing* occurrences in general English corpora, such as: "Mr. Kissinger said *the petition thing* never happened" confirms the hypothesis that *white balance thing* is not a term.

Examining the left-hand side context of *white balance* allows the translator to find collocations such as *accurate, daylight, cloudy, manual, automatic,* or *auto white balance*. A commonly applied process in English leads to the shifting of the POS of a word from noun to verb:

> But it will look white to you when you take the pictures because your brain will automatically **white balance** it.

More information can be extracted from a monolingual corpus about only one term. Once translators have listed possible terms, phraseology, derivational processes, etc., the time comes to find the equivalents in the target language (here: French).

## 5.3  Equivalents in the target language

The single general term 'balance' is usually translated into French by *équilibre*. Searching for *équilibre* in the French corpus on digital cameras does not yield any result. The solution lies in looking up the other component of the term, i.e. *white* and searching for *blanc* in the French corpus. Examining the context in which *blanc* appears, indicates that the equivalent of *white balance* is *balance des blancs*. In French *balance* usually means *scales*. The same search as for the English term must be done on the French term to find the French verbs that are used, or the adjectives and their position in French.

The collocates *high* or *low* are often found with the term *exposure*. Possible translations of *high* and *low* in French are usually *haut* and *bas*. In the case of *exposition* ( French for *exposure*), the adjectival collocates must be *forte* (*strong*) and *faible* (*weak*).

## 6.  Working with comparable and parallel (translation) corpora

In the field of computer science, postgraduate students had access to comparable corpora, as well as to a parallel (or translation) corpus (*Linux HowTo*'s translated into French). As their task was to analyze *SYSTRAN*'s translation problems and find the correct translations, they already had a list of terms and structures to look for.

### 6.1  Literal translations

*SYSTRAN* translates for example the term 'firewall machine' with *\*machine de mur pare-feu*, which is a literal and incorrect translation. Looking for the term in English leads to a search for the French translation in the corresponding paragraph. Luckily the parallel corpus comprises a definition of 'firewall'. Our concordancer allows the user to look for concordances, and then to have access to the English paragraph in which a selected occurrence has been found, as well as to the corresponding paragraph in French. Here is an extract of what can be found for 'firewall'*:*

> EN.     A firewall is a term used for a part of a car.  In cars, firewalls are physical objects that separate the engine from the passengers. They are meant to protect the passenger in case the car's engine catches fire while still providing the driver access to the engine's controls.
>
> A firewall in computers is a device that protects a private network from the public part (the internet as a whole).
>
> The firewall computer, from now on named 'firewall', (...)
>
> FR.     Firewall est un terme automobile.  Dans une voiture, un firewall  est  une pièce qui sépare le bloc-moteur du compartiment passagers. Il est prévu pour protéger les passagers en cas de feu au moteur en maintenant le controle de ce dernier par le conducteur.

> En informatique, un firewall est un péripherique qui protège la
> partie privée d'un réseau de la partie publique (InterNet en entier).
> L'ordinateur firewall, ci-après denomme 'firewall', (…)

As is often the case in CS French, the English term is not translated. Further searches in French corpora show however that French equivalents
for 'firewall' do exist, and are used depending on the genre of the text.
French computer scientists use the English word when they talk together,
or when they write or translate documents for other computer scientists.
In the case of a user manual that is written for a wider audience, the terms
*garde-barrière* or *coupe-feu* is more widely used.

## 6.2 Terminology problems

MT systems often have trouble with LSPs. Words commonly used in general English have a very different meaning in CS English. On the other
hand, translations that standardization organizations have tried to impose
are not used by the experts. These two phenomena can be illustrated with
the following sentence (EN) and its translation by *SYSTRAN* (SYS). Looking up for possible translations of 'hackers' and 'crackers' in the French
corpora (FR) shows that the first one is usually not translated, and that the
second one is translated as *pirates*, which bears the same negative conno-
tation as 'crackers' in CS English.

EN.    Hackers create, crackers destroy
SYS.   *Les intrus créent, des biscuits détruisent.
FR.    Les hackers créent, les pirates détruisent.

## 6.3 Verb structures and their arguments

Verbs are not widely described in LSPs although they play a most important role. As described in Kübler and Foucou (forthcoming), specialized
verbs may not exist in general language or have completely different
meanings.

EN.    Your BIOS may not allow you to boot to a Linux installed
there

FR.    Votre BIOS peut ne pas vous permettre de démarrer un
système Linux qui y serait installé

As said above, official standardization bodies sometimes suggest terms that are never used by the expert community. The French Commission for Computer Science Terminology tried to impose *amorcer* to translate *to boot*. A thorough search in our corpora, as well as on the Web, reveals that *amorcer* is not a possible translation. When a specialized verb has several possible translations, i.e. possible parasynonyms or different uses, parallel corpora provide the user with the possibility of checking each French translation the other way round. The first step consists in listing the possible French translations of the English verb for all its occurrences; syntactic structures and possible arguments must also be listed:

> 'to boot (strap)' = *lancer, démarrer, booter*, and not *\*amorcer*
> When Linux boots = Quand Linux se lance

The second step requires the translator to look for all the French verbs and check whether their equivalents in English are all the same. The question is: do all the French translations of 'to boot', i.e. *lancer, démarrer, booter*, match 'to boot' when looking at the French occurrence first, and then at the English corresponding paragraph? The answer for *lancer*, which is a possible translation of 'to boot', is negative for example:

> *lancer = launch | run, issue, type (a command)*

As *SYSTRAN* works with translation structures that are not complete, many problems arise concerning the verb structures and the types of arguments that are allowed in the different syntactic positions. Working with a parallel corpus and checking on comparable corpora gave the students a clearer picture of complex verb structures in French.

## 6.4  Using the Web

For the two projects, students were required to use the Web for different tasks. When they could not find a translation in the corpora, they had to formulate a hypothesis and try and confirm it by querying the Web. In the term 'focus brackets' for example, 'brackets' must not be translated by *parenthèses*. The correct translation is not in the digital cameras corpora. The translation of 'focus' can, however, be found: *mise au point*. Using a search engine on the Web for *mise au point* leads to the complete translation:

'focus brackets': repères de mise au point and not parenthèses ...

The number of Web pages that are found containing a specific term is a criterion that helps validate a term. In CS English, a 'Trojan horse' is a virus that works like the Trojan Horse in Homer. The hypothesis was that the French translation was used as well in CS French. The result of a query about *cheval de Troie* on a search engine deals almost exclusively with CS documents relating to viruses.

The Web is thus used to complement the usual context of a term that does not have enough context in the corpora or simply to complement corpora that cannot be updated every month in fast-evolving LSPs. A last example in CS and digital camera English, recently found on the Web, is the term *prosumer*, which is a contraction of "professional consumer", a blend.

# 7.  Conclusions and future prospects

This paper set out to show how combining various types of corpora and the Web can be introduced in translation training. Using comparable corpora in LSPs helps to overcome problems of 'artificiality' in parallel corpora. General language corpora are also necessary to test the degree of specialization of a term. Finally, the Web can be of great help in subject areas that change very quickly and in which neologisms are very common.

One of the questions that can be asked is the following: is this adequate training for future translator? Our department works with private companies in which our students carry out various kinds of tasks related to corpora, and from the feedback companies give the university, it seems that the answer is positive.

Translator training however leads to various kinds of jobs, such as: terminology extraction, manipulating documents using programming languages, building dictionaries for MT systems, localization, translating Web sites, technical writing. Learning to use corpora and corpus-query tools can give future translators the technical skills that were usually not associated with translation, but which seem to be more and more necessary, especially in technical translation.

Current work involves collecting more specialized corpora on various subjects. Postgraduate students have to collect corpora for their terminology and translation projects. They are therefore required to digitize them, when necessary, and tag them so that they can be integrated into our Web-based tools. Since the introduction of corpora in translator training radically changed the way students looked at languages, this led me to work on the development of a general methodological approach to introduce basic knowledge in linguistics and natural language processing and on how to use corpora in the fields of terminology and specialized translation.

# References

Foucou, Pierre-Yves and Natalie Kübler (2000) 'A Web-based Environment for Teaching Technical English', in Lou Burnard and Tony McEnery (eds) *Rethinking Language Pedagogy from a Corpus Perspective*, Frankfurt am Main: Peter Lang, 65-73.

Kübler, Natalie and Pierre-Yves Foucou (forthcoming) 'Teaching English Verbs with Bilingual Corpora: Examples in the Computer Science Area', in Sylviane Granger (ed) *Corpus-based Approaches to Contrastive Linguistics and Translation Studies*, Amsterdam: Rodopi.

Maia, Belinda (2000) 'Making Corpora: A Learning Process', in Silvia Bernardini and Federico Zanettin (eds) *Corpus Use and Learning to Translate*, Bologna: CLUEB, 47-60.

Pearson, Jennifer (1998) *Terms in Context*, Amsterdam and Philadelphia: John Benjamins.

Sinclair, John (1991) *Corpus, Concordance, Collocation,* Oxford: Oxford University Press.

# "Some Languages are more Equal than Others"

## Training Translators in Terminology and Information Retrieval using Comparable and Parallel Corpora

BELINDA MAIA

*The use of corpora to verify how words are used in context can be particularly useful in areas of LSP and terminology. The very possibility of examining terms in texts that deal with the subject matter under discussion makes it easier for the terminologist – and also the translator – to understand the concepts behind the terms used. However, whereas one can follow the advice of Pearson (1998) for monolingual texts in English, it is less easy to find comparable or parallel texts which are reliable, of an equal level of complexity and which offer the same information value. This paper will look at efforts made to find and use text corpora in English and Portuguese to further terminology work in various areas, the problems that arise and how they can, or cannot, be solved.*

## 1. Introduction

Some years ago, at the first conference on *Corpus Use and Learning to Translate*, I described ways of encouraging students to form mini-corpora on specialized subjects within the parameters of normal translation classes (Maia 2000). As well as using printed texts and CD-ROMs, the Internet had opened up the opportunity to find and download texts on virtually anything, and first experiments showed that making mini-corpora was a good way for students to find and collect vocabulary about unfamiliar subjects, and at the same time learn how to judge the style, complexity and information value of different texts. Over the last few years we have been pursuing this methodology at the University of Porto, moving towards more serious terminology work. Here I focus on some of the problems encountered in training translators to produce specialized corpora in English and Portuguese for information retrieval and term extraction.

One of the most significant constraints has been the restricted availability of quality texts in Portuguese. In developing corpora for translation purposes it is of vital importance to find good original texts, written by native speakers – and, as far as possible, good translations of them into the other language. What first just seemed a problem of finding Portuguese texts in electronic form – the non-English speaking world still has to catch up in putting texts on CD-ROM and the Internet – has proved to be a more general one, also at the level of printed texts. The *Economist* of October 28th – November 3rd 2000 led with "A Constitution for the European Union". Article 2 of this Constitution read as follows:

> **Languages.** English, French and German shall have equal standing as the sole official languages of the Union institutions.

With the following footnote:

> This shifts the main burden of other translation to member states that want it.

This proposal to restrict the production of translations into 'less prestigious' languages seems indicative of an attitude which is widespread, with severe consequences for those wishing to compile corpora for translation purposes.

## 2.  Selecting texts

Ever since the earliest attempts at corpus building, selecting the right texts to include has been a problem, whether the objective is the ideal representative corpus for general lexicography, or specialized corpora such as the parallel or comparable ones required for translation and terminology purposes.

### 2.1  Parallel corpora

Collecting parallel corpora means acquiring both original texts and their translations in electronic form. Applications of parallel corpora to translation and terminology work have included:

    a)  Providing teaching materials
    b)  Studying the process of translation
    c)  Saving the material for information purposes and for future reference

a) The use of parallel texts as teaching materials is a time-honoured method not only in teaching translation, but foreign languages in general. However, given limited time and space, and the scarcity of off-the-shelf resources, parallel corpora developed for teaching purposes have rarely gone beyond a small selection of texts which, for obvious pedagogic reasons, have not concentrated in depth on specialized areas.

b) Studying the translation process is probably the preferred use of parallel corpora by academics, whether their interests are linguistic, literary or pedagogic. However these interests often lead them to focus on translation anomalies rather than on correct parallels, and to choose texts for study where interesting anomalies are to be found.

c) To be a reliable source of information for translators and terminologists, on the other hand, parallel texts must provide good translations, and use terms correctly. It is sensible for translators to keep such texts for future use, and this is increasingly done through computerised translation memory systems. If a translation memory program is available, encouraging students to create well-selected specialized parallel corpora is one way of finding a practical use for it in the teaching context. Otherwise, the creation of memories which are large enough to produce the savings in time and energy the software designers claim for them is unlikely to be a priority.

Collecting parallel texts, particularly non-literary ones, is however not easy. Apart from the difficulty of getting permission to use texts which are in copyright (Pearson 1998: 1), there are many factors which may limit their reliability. For instance:

- the original text may itself be a translation, or written by an author with limited competence in the source language
- the translation may have been done in a hurry, and consequently contain errors or reflect the textual and syntactic structure of the original too closely
- the translation may have been done by a non-native speaker of the target language, or by a native-speaker without training in translation
- the original and/or the translation may have been subjected to editorial interference, not always beneficially

Only when both the original texts and the translations are 'good' can parallel corpora provide reliable instruments for translation and terminology purposes.

## 2.2  Comparable corpora

Comparable corpora are "collections of individual monolingual corpora" which use "the same or similar sampling procedures and categories for each language but contain completely different texts" (McEnery and Wilson, 1996: 57). It is usually easier to create good comparable corpora than parallel ones, since more monolingual than bilingual texts are available, even when – as desirable – only original texts by native-speaker authors are used. The main difficulties lie in establishing the categories and procedures for sampling, and then finding texts in both languages that match these criteria.

Specialized monolingual corpora are useful tools in the areas of genre and style analysis (Biber, 1988; Swales, 1990; Bhatia, 1993; Stubbs, 1996; Biber, Conrad and Reppen, 1998), LSP teaching (Halliday and Martin, 1993; Martin and Veal, 1998; Howcroft, 1999), and terminology extraction (Pearson, 1998). While generally focussing on English, these studies provide models that can also be applied to other languages. However it is not always easy to compile comparable corpora along these lines, since the texts available in the two languages may be very different.

## 2.3  Finding the texts

One is obviously hesitant to refer to the results of students' efforts to collect texts of a particular kind as 'corpora'. There may seem to be little relation between their rough-and-ready collections of raw texts and the well-selected, carefully-processed, encoded and annotated corpora prepared by linguists. My argument, however, is that the process of compiling such collections is educational, even where the product is not fully satisfactory.

Where the objective is that of obtaining information about a specialized field and extracting terminology, the first problem to be faced is that of finding appropriate texts from both languages to include in the corpus, be this parallel or comparable in nature. There are four main possible sources, each of which has its own limits.

- *Encyclopædias, dictionaries and general reference texts.* Our experience in using these to introduce students to a specialised subject and its terms in English and Portuguese has not been happy. While English texts on almost anything can be found on the Internet, starting with the Encyclopædia Britannica, much less is available in Portuguese. And while recent years have seen considerable efforts to produce such texts in Portuguese on CD-ROM, these are often translations (wholly or in part) of English originals.
- *Journalism.* At first sight, there would appear to be many advantages in using texts from newspapers, which are available in enormous quantities on the Web and on CD-ROM, even for minority languages.[1] They provide a wide range of subject matter and are lexically 'up-to-date'. One disadvantage, however, is that most international news agencies distribute original material in English, and translations may be done in a hurry. Thus while local news items in the Portuguese press typically adopt an AVS or V(S) sentence structure, we find a much higher proportion of English SVO structures in the international news, with the conventions of information structure in Portuguese subordinated to those of English.
- *Textbooks.* Supposedly good sources of terminology are school and university textbooks. But Portuguese textbooks are often bad translations, so that, for instance, the cultural references for exercises often continue to refer to American reality (Howcroft 1999). At university level, where there may be a scarcity of textbooks in the students' own language, prescribed texts are often in English.[2] Howcroft argues that these conditions contribute to a learning deficit – an opinion also voiced by a professor at our local medical faculty. Thanks to the aggressive marketing techniques of international publishers, and others who control access to information and culture, publishers in non-English-speaking countries may be reluctant to invest in locally-authored projects, finding it cheaper and quicker to produce low-quality translations for those who are unable to read the originals.
- *Specialist literature.* Relatively little specialist literature may be

---

[1] See, for example, the 180-million word CETEMPublico corpus in Portuguese at http://www.portugues.mct.pt/

[2] Brazilian Portuguese translations, of which many more are available, are often rejected on the grounds that they are poorly translated or use different terminology.

available in the local language. In Portugal, particularly outside the humanities, one hears it argued that it is better for students to have to cope in English, particularly when specializing near the end of their studies, since no engineer, scientist, doctor or technician without English can hope to function in the global marketplace. A parallel argument runs as follows. So much is first published in English that, with certain fields evolving so fast, waiting for a translation would simply hold up research – particularly as the translation may never come. And once one gets the research done, if one does not publish the results in English, they will be condemned to international obscurity: problems of international recognition contribute not a little to inferiority complexes among non-English-speaking academics. Consequently, Portuguese academia does not always give due value to its mother tongue. However a few high-level scientific texts do get translated by local academics, and these parallel texts are probably the best resources available for terminological work.

## 3.   Work in progress

### 3.1  Undergraduate projects

Projects involving the collection of specialized texts and bilingual terminology have been introduced into the first year of specialization in translation  (the third of the four-year undergraduate course). The work has to be done outside class, and students are encouraged to use friends or family to help them with the specialized subject chosen. Due to time factors and to students' relatively low level of sophistication, these projects are limited in scope: previous experience is limited to the general vocabulary of language classes, and students tend to think they only need to know the general aspects of the language and can look the rest up in the dictionary.

Many students choose concrete objects like tools for gardening, carpentry, ironwork, and jewelry work. They enlist the help of people who work in the area, visit shops that sell these objects, with the aim of producing glossaries into which they insert drawings and photographs. They find relatively few texts, often catalogues with explanations of the tools' use that can serve as a basis for definitions. Such catalogues can usually be found in English and Spanish, but not always in Portuguese.  Among the questions raised here are:

- When does a text of this kind become a suitable candidate for a specialized corpus?
- How, under these circumstances, does one avoid the simple adoption of cognates in English or Spanish, which are often false friends, as Portuguese equivalents (also by the Portuguese public)?

Other students start their work with an English language glossary they have found on the Internet – or elsewhere. They too find it quite easy to get accompanying texts in English, but almost impossible to find anything in Portuguese. In contrast, others have worked on natural species, such as sharks, finding lots of encyclopedia articles – but often very repetitive ones. However, some brighter students discover ways of using their corpora that go beyond simple glossaries of terms. In one project on "Earthquakes and Volcanoes", the student not only extracted lists of technical words from her specialized corpus, but also of metaphorical expressions related to this area. Another used a corpus of parallel texts from the European Commission to make a collection of functional expressions like 'in accordance with', 'notwithstanding' etc., and their respective translations.

## 3.2 Postgraduate projects

Recently two students took up the challenge to work in the area of terminology for their dissertations, on the rather shaky basis of a Master's course in "Translation Studies", of which three-quarters of the curriculum is devoted to literary translation. Their inspiration came from the remaining quarter, which included a seminar on "Information Technology and Translation" dealing *inter alia* with the use of corpora for various types of research, and involved a project proposed by individuals working for the translation services of the EU and for the União Latina in Lisbon, in relation to the terminology of steel and concrete structures in Portuguese and English.

The original intention for these dissertations was to take the English and Portuguese versions of the Eurocodes for civil engineering, align the texts, extract the terminology, correct and check any problems with an expert, and then produce a database in Trados Multiterm. This all seemed very straightforward, even if the engineering expert balked somewhat at the idea of definitions in Portuguese. However, we agreed that if the Eurocodes corpus was supplemented by other texts in the same area, it should be possible to find suitable definitions: after all, any termbank is expected to provide definitions, and to indicate their sources.

It was agreed that the students would each carry out their research in a way that suited their personal interests and attitudes (both were professional translators, and one also taught English language and translation). The first practical step each took was to scan those parts of the Eurocodes that were not already in digital form, and to align the English and Portuguese texts using Trados WinAlign. As this work proceeded, it became obvious that whatever the quality of the texts and their terminology, there was hardly a definition in sight (except in the shape of mathematical formulæ, which seemed to coincide anyhow). However, with the help of *Wordsmith Tools* (Scott 1996), and the suggestions of Pearson (1998), each made wordlists and extracted lists of possible terms from them, and generated concordances for these.

Each then drew up conceptual frameworks within which to organize their terms. Since the Eurocodes texts provided little help here, they found what they could in the Universal Decimal System, engineering thesauri and other specialized glossaries. They had the run of the Faculty of Engineering library, but found little in the way of introductory texts providing definitions and explanations – except in English. One student, who was unlucky in her attempts to contact specialists, decided to show why it is impossible to produce a termbank to ISO standards without the help of an expert. The other, after preparing a good deal of material, went to greater lengths to find expert help. She made contact with several Portuguese engineers, who were very encouraging and provided further bibliography. One even sent her all his personal teaching material in Portuguese, some of which she scanned in as a further resource for term extraction. Finally, with weeks to go before handing in her dissertation, she went to see a professor in the Faculty of Engineering, who was sufficiently impressed to spend several hours going through her work and answering her questions, and made drawings and diagrams to help her.

The results of these students' efforts – apart from the dissertations themselves – were glossaries of terms extracted from the corpus, complemented by items from other texts, along with schemes of the conceptual areas covered. They also inserted some terms into Multiterm databases, which now need time, patience and more expert advice to complete.

We are now in a position to take stock of the situation and see what we have learnt. Of the two institutions behind the original proposal, the União Latina in Lisbon had previously produced only printed glossaries, containing little information beyond the terms and their translations, and perhaps a glossary was all they really wanted. Our EU contacts hoped to obtain a Trados translation memory and termbank which would be compatible with the other instruments they were using. The element that seemed to be missing from both calculations was the need, or ability, of humanities-trained terminologists – and women to boot – to comprehend what all these terms actually meant. We are now trying to ensure that all glossaries from student projects are based on an understanding of their subject-matter, whether derived from reading or direct experience.

## 4. Corpora and the need to know

How much do translators or terminologists actually need to know about the subject matter of the texts they are working on? How much of the triangle of 'res', concept, and word (Figure 1) do they need to understand? The expert works from the 'res' and the concept towards the term or word. The translator-in-a-hurry often has to make do with the term or word taken from some bilingual dictionary or glossary; however, the translator who systematically adopts this solution will never be a good professional. The terminologist must try and synchronize all three aspects, and the translator can learn from that experience.

It is obvious that students first have to reach a certain level of general language use – in both their own and foreign languages – before they can embark on anything more specialized. It is equally obvious that in real

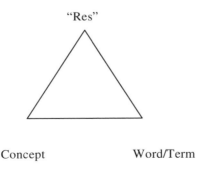

Figure 1. Relationship between word/term, concept and "res"

life, the translator has to fake a lot of specialized knowledge (Robinson, 1998: Chapter 7). Nonetheless, translators need to learn how to specialize, and from this point of view it does not matter if the subjects dealt with at university never come up in their future careers. In collecting specialized texts – particularly of the encyclopedic or textbook variety – students are obliged to read and hopefully understand more of the subject dealt with: consequently, they may find translating texts in that area more interesting. In extracting terminology from a corpus, they become aware of the nature of terminology and the need for translators to be rigorous in their choice of words.

The market tendency is towards specialization in translation. The methodology involved in making corpora and extracting terminology should be part of the teaching curriculum – not an optional extra – particularly given the pressure on translators to use computer-assisted tools. If students have this training, translation memories and terminological databases will make sense to them, and they will be better prepared for a market that has never been kind. In Porto we have now started a Master's degree in "Terminology and Translation", explicitly focussed on non-literary texts, in which teachers of engineering, history and geography will help students to produce specialized corpora and termbanks.[3] Despite their tendency to favour English as an international language, it has not been difficult to enlist these teachers' cooperation: they seem more aware of the problem of poor terminology than many teachers of languages. The number of similar courses elsewhere in Europe is growing,[4] and the fact that we have had 42 candidates for 20 places suggests that the need is also felt by the professional translators at whom the new degree is aimed. We hope they will not be disappointed.

# References

Bhatia, Vijay K. (1993) *Analysing Genre,* London and New York: Longman.
Biber, Douglas (1988) *Variation Across Speech and Writing,* Cambridge: Cambridge University Press.

---

[3] Master's in "Terminology and Translation" at Universidade do Porto - see http://www.letras.up.pt/translat/i_mes.html

[4] See e.g. the Master's in "English-Spanish Technical Translation" at Universitat Rovira I Virgili – see: http://www.fut.es/~apym/masters/m1_2.html

------ Susan Conrad and Randi Reppen (1998) *Corpus Linguistics: Investigating Language Structure and Use,* Cambridge: Cambridge University Press.

Halliday, MAK and James R. Martin (1993) *Writing Science: Literacy and Discursive Power,* London and Washington: The Falmer Press.

Howcroft, Susan Jean (1999) *English for Science and Technology: A Computer Corpus-based Analysis of English Science and Technology Texts for Application in Higher Education,* Universidade de Aveiro: Unpublished PhD Thesis.

Maia, Belinda (2000) 'Making Corpora: A Learning Process', in Silvia Bernardini and Federico Zanettin (eds) *Corpus Use and Learning to Translate,* Bologna: CLUEB, 47-60.

Martin, James R. and Robert Veal (eds) (1998) *Reading Science: Critical and Functional Perspectives on Discourses of Science,* London and New York: Routledge.

McEnery, Tony and Andrew Wilson (1996) *Corpus Linguistics,* Edinburgh: Edinburgh University Press.

Pearson, Jennifer (1998) *Terms in Context,* Amsterdam and Philadelphia: John Benjamins.

Robinson, Douglas (1998) *Becoming a Translator: An Accelerated Course,* London and New York: Routledge.

Scott, Mike (1996) *Wordsmith Tools,* Oxford: Oxford University Press.

Stubbs, Michael (1996) *Text and Corpus Analysis: Computer-assisted Studies of Language and Culture,* Oxford: Blackwell.

Swales, John M. (1990) *Genre Analysis,* Cambridge: Cambridge University Press.

# Translators and Disposable Corpora

KRISTA VARANTOLA

*This article will focus on the use of disposable, ad hoc corpora in translation. The study is based on a workshop experiment using the Web as a corpus resource. The main emphasis is on the compilation of these corpora and their analysis tools. A distinction is made between competence and performance in translation. It is pointed out that disposable corpora can be structurally simple but nevertheless very useful performance-enhancing tools in translation. A simple corpus structure does not, however, imply that there are no design criteria for these corpora. It is claimed that the knowledge of how to compile corpora and use them is an essential part of modern translational competence. A tentative list of corpus management skills is sketched at the end of the article.*

## 1. Introduction

This article will focus on the use of ad hoc corpora, their design criteria and their analysis tools in the process of translating. The study is based on a workshop experiment conducted at the Department of Translation Studies, University of Tampere, using the Web as a resource for comparable corpora.

Ad hoc comparable corpora are typically collected for a single translation assignment, i.e. to help in the translation of particular texts.[1] Since these ad hoc corpora are collected to satisfy a transitory need, they are not primarily aimed at forming a part of a permanent text corpus. For this reason, they should rather be categorized as virtual corpora (cf. Ahmad *et al.* 1994), in other words, as some kind of here-now-gone-tomorrow corpora. I will therefore call them disposable comparable corpora.

However, before going deeper in the subject, I would like to comment on a terminological issue that will prevent confusion over terms used. At one time it was customary in translation contexts to categorize text collections either as translation text collections or translation corpora, or as

---

[1] Translation is here used in its widest sense and refers both to the actual translation of a source text, and to text design and text production in the target language, as well as to the revision of an already translated text with the help of relevant, new comparable text data in the target language.

parallel text collections or parallel text corpora. Translation corpora then referred to corpora consisting of original and translated texts in given languages, whereas parallel corpora described text collections of 'authentic' texts in the given languages. These were texts that dealt with the same subject matter or topic in all the languages but were not translations of each other. However, since then, the prevailing terminology has changed so that electronic translation corpora are now generally referred to as parallel corpora, and former parallel corpora are called comparable corpora. In this study I shall adhere to this prevailing terminology.

The basic design criterion for a disposable corpus arises from the source text or source material to be worked on. It is the source material that defines the types of texts to be included in the disposable corpus. The corpora do not need to be sophisticated in terms of syntactic or semantic tagging. In fact, they can be structurally very simple, text-only corpora, but they can nevertheless be very useful in the actual decision-making process in translation.

Yet, a simple corpus structure does not imply that similar subject matter is the only design criterion. Quite the opposite, I think that it is necessary to study in depth the types of criteria that have to be taken into consideration when compiling disposable corpora. I would even go a step further and claim that the knowledge of how to compile and use corpora is an essential part of modern translational competence and should therefore be dealt with in the training of prospective professional translators.

## 2.  The Internet as a corpus resource

Today we can claim that the World Wide Web provides practically unlimited access to electronic texts that can be used in compiling individual disposable corpora for translation. Moreover, we can claim that this statement begins to be true even for languages other than English.

For this reason, the problem is no longer the availability of electronic corpus data at your fingertips, but rather the relevance, adequacy, reliability and the analysis of this context-sensitive corpus material. The real issues lie in finding the right material for the translation in question and knowing how to analyze and use it. In other words, it is necessary for the translator to be highly competent in textual and stylistic analysis and, in addition, to be computer- and software literate at a fairly advanced level.

As an umbrella term, we could use *corpus management in translation* and by this refer to the knowledge and skills needed in the compilation and use of corpus information for individual translation assignments. Corpus management, in turn, can be seen as an aspect of lexical knowledge management. Compilation and analysis tools used in corpus building and corpus use would then belong to the translator's toolbox and coexist in a translator's workstation together with other translation software. Translation memory programs, term tools and machine translation software are examples of this type of software. In addition, the workstation would have collections of or access to electronic dictionaries, term and knowledge banks, permanent and non-permanent corpus collections and other sources of reference.

The corpus compilation facility in a translator's workstation would thus give a new performance tool to translators, a tool that they would benefit from in their lexical and textual knowledge management.

In the context of technical communication, knowledge management has been defined as access to the information you need to have. Technical communication, in turn, has been defined "as transferring knowledge from those who know to those who need to know" (cf. Carliner 1999: 85). Dictionaries, glossaries and other reference sources serve a very similar purpose during actual translation work. They are used as information sources for decision-making. Translators consult dictionaries to obtain information on the form, meaning and use of words and expressions, and this information becomes knowledge when the acquired information is applied in an appropriate context. In addition, translators turn to encyclopaedic or domain-specific knowledge sources and subject specialists when they need encyclopaedic information. How could disposable corpora, then, contribute to this information acquisition process?

## 3. Competence and performance in translation

It can be claimed that a translator's proficiency depends on both translational competence and on performance skills that match this competence, and that the actual translation process is essentially a decision-making process (the ensuing discussion is largely based on Varantola 1994). In addition to proficiency-related aspects, translation work is naturally influenced by factors originating outside the translation process but a more profound survey of these factors is beyond the scope of the present article. It is enough to keep in mind that the quality of the translation product can depend on such different factors as how coherent or incoherent the source material is, how feasible the deadlines are or whether the client is committed to helping the translator when necessary. The outcome can also be influenced by political or cultural norms or other restrictive fringe conditions which might result in deliberate manipulations of the translated text (cf. e.g. Lefevere 1992, Venuti 1995).

**Competence**. Yet, if we restrict ourselves to the translators and their proficiency, we can continue by claiming that translational competence reflects a conscious theory- or theories-based approach that is essentially a decision-making process about strategic choices. How one acquires this theoretical strategic knowledge is another matter. I personally believe that it is possible to acquire a strategic competence in a number of ways, through practice, through academic studies, or through both.

In non-literary translation, the translator often needs to determine which kind of text will best suit the target audience. The translator will thus have to decide, for instance, whether a manual or an instruction booklet needs to be re-targeted for a new audience, i.e., adjusted in order to meet the new users' information needs and cultural expectations. Today, it is often also necessary to localize or globalize a text, depending on the purpose for which the particular version of the text is being produced. Very often these types of translations are not the result of the work by an individual translator, but products based on team work and policy decisions.

Yet regardless of whether we are dealing with literary or non-literary translation, there are, at this level, few decisions made by the translator that can be classified as right or wrong strategic choices. Instead, it might be more appropriate to discuss these choices in terms of adequate-to-inadequate strategies. In the case of literary translation, discussion about strategies may reflect how well the chosen strategies suit the tastes of the audience or how well the translation is received by the reviewers. There is also ample evidence of how the prevailing cultural or political atmosphere affects the translators' scope for manoeuvre.

These issues belong to the language-independent, competence side of translation, and are issues that can only be evaluated by means of a scale of adequate to inadequate strategic choices in a particular context, at a particular time, in a particular cultural setting, and for a particular audience. In addition, translational competence covers such aspects as the translator's ability to detect the potential translation problems in an assignment and the know-how of ways to solve them.

**Performance**. When discussing the performance side of translation, actual language use, linguistic and stylistic choices immediately begin to play a major role. The translator's linguistic proficiency in general, his or her ability to use language fluently and correctly, is of prime importance. Even at this level, our evaluation scale is sometimes that of adequate-to-inadequate, but probably more often we use a more normative scale of right-to-wrong, particularly when assessing L1-L2 translation (native-to-foreign language translation).

## 4. Mismatch between competence and performance

Translators consult reference sources for various reasons. They may search for a lexical equivalent either in their L1 or in the L2, or they may be looking for a special field term, grammatical or stylistic information, usage examples, encyclopaedic information, etc. It is often difficult to say what exactly the information need is, because in many cases it is an integrated continuum of information acquisition that can be used at the actual decision-making stage. Figure 1 aims to illustrate this continuum:

| equivalent | grammatical collocation | lexical collocation | examples | idiomatic usage | longer passage | paragraph structure | text structure | stylistic information | encyclopaedic information |
|---|---|---|---|---|---|---|---|---|---|

**Figure 1.** The continuum of information needs [Varantola]

If translators do not find satisfactory solutions for these types of information needs, a mismatch may arise between translators' competence and their performance. In other words, translators do not find the information they need for their decision making although they are well aware of what the problem is. This problem can be lexical or terminological, but it can also embrace longer passages and stylistic issues. On the other hand, it can be a multiple or fuzzy problem that is difficult or impossible to pinpoint (See also Varantola 2000).

## 5. Disposable translation corpora as performance-enhancing tools

It is obvious that the greatest promise that the Web and other on-line resources can offer to translators is to enhance their chances of finding satisfactory solutions to their translation problems. It is in this vein that we can study disposable, ad hoc corpora and regard them as performance-enhancing tools in translation or, more precisely, as decision-making tools for lexical and textual knowledge management in translation.

# 6.  Previous observations about corpus use in translation

A previous workshop on corpus use showed that translation students had many reservations and doubts about compiling and using disposable corpora (See Varantola 2000). Their main concern was about cost efficiency. Corpora were found to be useful but very cumbersome to collect. We must, however, keep in mind that this experiment dates back to the mid-90's when the Web was often very slow and the quality of the information retrieved was often unsatisfactory. The benefits of corpora and the adequacy of the solutions found in them thus greatly depended on the text type, style and subject matter of the translation assignment when the Web was the only available source for corpus compilation.

Other main observations from that experiment were that corpora should be used together with dictionaries and that dictionaries and corpora should be seen as complementary and not as overlapping tools. The students also pointed out that user skills and advanced search strategies are crucial in corpus utilization. The solely positive comments dealt with the unexpected benefits of corpus use. The students made a number of finds – which they called serendipitous – through fuzzy corpus searches mainly by means of concordancing with contextually relevant search words. They also found adequate answers for questions they did not think of asking, such as good cues of how to formulate ideas in an idiomatic fashion, because the corpus texts provided them with collocational information stretching over whole texts. To summarize, besides answering explicit questions, corpus information also proved useful even in discovering and solving implicit translation problems.

# 7.  The 'new' experiment

This new experiment was conducted according to principles similar to the first study, but a few years later. This time, however, the assignments were group assignments and also 'real' assignments in the sense that the groups had to deliver a finished translation to the customer and were also paid for their work. The emphasis in this workshop was on defining search criteria for relevant corpus texts. The participants determined search criteria by identifying target group needs and text-type characteristics. The corpus tool package used was *Wordsmith Tools* (Scott 1996). Each group received hands-on tuition on how to download texts from the Web and how to apply *Wordsmith Tools* in corpus analysis.

*Work group assignments.* Four of the target texts were based on Finnish-to-English text production and one was a translation into Finnish from English source material. Again, translation is used here in its widest sense (see endnote 1), to cover both the traditional source text – target text perception of the translation process, as well as the increasingly common tasks of text production and localization on the basis of mono- or multi-lingual source material.

The assignments and their descriptions were as follows:

Finnish-English:
Group 1. A summary of the mediation procedure and practices in Finnish legislation. An informative text for EU purposes.
Group 2. A brochure text of an educational game designed for dyslexic children. Mixed scientific and general style.
Group 3. A translation of a Finnish instruction booklet for HIV-positive patients. Mixed medical jargon and general, neutral style.
Group 4. A revision of an earlier medical-field translation, an instruction booklet for people suffering from hypertension. An informative and operative text. Mixed medical and simplistic general style.

English-Finnish:
Group 5. A text dealing with an evaluation of the EU rural development programme – LEADER. An informative, operative, and instructional text dealing with procedural unification.

# 8. Competence-related decisions at the pre-translation stage

I shall give a few examples of the type of competence-based strategic choices that were made before starting corpus compilation. Groups 3 and 4 concluded that their target groups would be international and heterogeneous with varying educational backgrounds. In the majority of cases, English would not be the native language of these target groups. The audience would thus be the non-Finnish speaking immigrant population in Finland. The target texts should therefore be easy-to-understand and not specialized or academic in approach.

Group 2 aimed at producing a text that would be technically and

terminologically convincing for speech therapists and other professionals, but also clear and easy to understand. Groups 1 and 5, on the other
hand, did not have any specifically defined user groups in mind. Their
concern was to make the texts informative and comprehensible. Group 1
needed to explain Finnish legal practices to an international audience and
Group 5 aimed at making obscure EU prose comprehensible to a Finnish
audience.

## 9.   Problems perceived at the pre-corpus stage

Before starting corpus compilation, the groups discussed the types of problems they would encounter during the actual translation process and the
type of corpus reference material that would be helpful in solving these
performance-related problems The groups based their discussions on the
source-text material and their analysis of the target text audiences. The
results of the discussions gave preliminary search criteria for the corpus
material. These criteria can be divided into two main categories:

1.      Linguistic and textual issues:
   • terminological information, e.g. culture-specific legal terminology,
     specialized terminology, less technical medical terminology or fuzzy
     EU terminology (e.g. *added value* (in two senses), *animation unit,
     internal rate of return, pluriactivity, specifications*) and terminol-
     ogy from a number of fields (in this case economy, cattle raising,
     demography)
   • stylistic information, e.g. stylistic conventions for instruction and
     marketing texts, general informative styles
   • coping with problematic source text material (e.g. the EU material
     on the LEADER programme written in complex and partly incom-
     prehensible Euese, in this case English with strong French influence
     and overtones, long and cumbersome sentence structures and fuzzy
     EU expressions)

2.      Information retrieval issues:
   • coping with the expected information overflow, in this case with
     the wealth of on-line information about AIDS or HIV

At this stage, tentative design criteria were used to define the types and
sources of texts to be collected and to suggest concrete heuristic strategies

of how to find these texts:

General definitions of relevant texts to be included:
- case studies, instruction booklets, general advice texts, stylistically relevant texts (e.g. newspaper articles)
- texts written by native English speakers, preferably of European origin

Concrete heuristic strategies:
- material from the home pages of relevant research institutes and associations (e.g. heart associations, pharmaceutical company home pages)
- specialised texts (e.g. from conference proceedings)
- web addresses referred to in the source text
- Finnish on-line EU texts dealing with the LEADER project and rural development issues in general using such search parameters as "LEADER", AND/NEAR, "EU" to ensure relevancy of the texts

# 10. Corpus details

## 10.1 Concrete compilation strategies

It is not easy to find relevant and only relevant corpus material and very much depends on the inventiveness of the search strategies. The following examples will show concretely how two of the groups tried to cope with this issue.

Group 4 used medical terminology and vocabulary present in the source material for the first round of search words. Examples of such search words are *hypertension, blood pressure, high blood pressure, animal fat, arrhythmia, beta blockers, obesity* AND *hypertension*. After compiling a pilot corpus with search words of this type, this group did a key-word search on the downloaded texts to obtain new search words for a second round of corpus compilation.

Group 5 occasionally used English search words + *domain:fi* to restrict the searches to Finnish sources. This helped them to find locally used EU guides, instruction booklets, governmental evaluation pages, etc. They also checked every text candidate for relevancy before including it in their corpus.

## 10.2    Problems in corpus compilation

All groups had problems during compilation which concerned the accessibility and the reliability of the information found.

***Accessibility:***
- many sources charged a fee
- too many sources found were U.S. sources. The groups would have preferred to include a higher number of European, particularly British English, texts to ensure a better balanced corpus
- the medical texts were often too short, frequently occurring as mere lists of drugs
- many search words were too general to begin with (e.g. AIDS- ) the result being a non-manageable overflow of information
- too few texts were available in Finnish
- the Finnish material was often stylistically inadequate and written in non-standard Finnish

***Reliability:***
- some texts, both English and Finnish texts, had so many misprints that it made the corpus compilers very suspicious about their quality
- a number of textual details and characteristics occasionally made the compilers suspicious about the authenticity of the authors

## 10.3  Quantitative characteristics of the corpora

The size of the corpora used by the groups in their respective translation tasks varied a great deal in size (See Table 1).

The results in Table 1 seem to indicate that corpus size alone does not determine corpus adequacy when collecting disposable corpora. Instead, the adequacy of the corpus totally depends on the quality of information the translator is able to extract from it. We can thus claim that the primary criterion for corpus adequacy is its ability to provide information that satisfies the information needs of the translator. This means that only the translator can decide whether the corpus is a satisfactory corpus for any particular translation assignment. In this sense, the use of disposable corpora is a truly interactive operation.

Corpus size can be increased on demand. The users can decide what type of additional material is needed. This need arises in a situation  in

| Group/ Source material | Tokens | Types | Comment |
|---|---|---|---|
| 1. Mediation procedure legislation (FI-EN) | 159,739 | 8102 | |
| 2. Brochure, educational games (FI-EN) | 12,583 | ---- | Scope of translation narrow |
| 3. HIV instruction booklet (FI-EN) | 72,536 | 5472 | |
| 4. Revision of an instruction booklet on hypertension (EN-EN) | 107,567 | 8168 | |
| 5. Evaluation of an EU rural development programme (FI-EN) | ~60,000 | ~15,000 | Mostly Finnish texts. No of types reflects both the inflectional nature of Finnish and the variety of the texts collected |

**Table 1.** Corpus characteristics

which the users have not found what they are looking for. Nevertheless, the adequacy of the corpus greatly depends on the analytical skills of the user both at the compilation and the utilization stage. We can claim that the corpus is fully adequate if it satisfactorily answers all the questions that the user puts to it. On the other hand, we must concede defeat in the sense that we will never be able to determine whether a corpus also answers all the questions that the users have not thought of asking although they should have done so. Yet, I think that we can safely say that if experienced users make a number of serendipitous finds in a corpus, they have most probably succeeded very well in the compilation task. In such cases they have been able to find high quality material that closely corresponds to the source material they are using to produce the target text.

# 11.    Application of corpus information

In this particular case study, some groups succeeded better than others with corpus compilation and corpus utilization. Group 4, which was collecting patient information about hypertension, decided to rely on corpus evidence and consequently replace a number of special medical terms by more transparent general-style expressions. Some other less obviously accountable lexical changes also depended on corpus evidence and their frequency of occurrence. For example, the group decided to opt for the following lexical choices:

- patient *over* subject
- irregular heart rhythm over arrhythmia
- over-the-counter medicine *over* non-prescription drug
- drugless treatment *over* non-drug treatment

- premature death *over* untimely death
- elderly *over* older people
- elevated blood pressure *over* raised blood pressure

This group also claimed that corpus evidence helped them to make radical stylistic changes in their revision task.

Group 3, which was working on the instruction booklet for those who are HIV-positive, used their corpus in a similar manner. They decided that *asymptomatic* or *seroconversion* were not commonly used terms and generally recognized concepts because they occurred in only 8 out of the 33 texts. Thus, where it was necessary to use these terms in the target text, they needed to be accompanied by definitions. *Opportunistic* and *lymph nodes*, however, appeared in a great number of texts and must therefore be generally known. Nevertheless, *lymph nodes* were also referred to as glands  (*swollen glands*) in the corpus and this should be kept in mind when checking the consistency of the terminology in the target text.

Group 3 also resorted to sophisticated, indirect deduction chains when searching for corpus information. They realized that *mucosa* or *mucose membrane*, which they had thought of using in their translation, were not used in their corpus consisting of popularized medical texts. But because the concepts behind these terms are central to AIDS, there must be other ways of referring to them in popularized English texts. To find these expressions, they used *transmit* as a search word and found that *lining* and *tissue*  were the words that were used in general instructional material. The same was true about LAS which could not be found in the corpus material. Concordancing with *stage/s* revealed that *mild illness/severe illness* were the expressions used to describe the different stages of the illness.

## 12. *Wordsmith Tools* in translation

### 12.1 The tools

The groups experimented with the various *Wordsmith* 'tools' and discussed their uses in their reports. Many of the functions were used in a very innovative fashion.

- the concordancer was used to gain collocational and contextual information and it proved to be very useful in those tasks
- the concordancer was also used to retrieve longer stretches of text which were used to find information on text construction and cohesive mechanisms

- word lists and word frequency proved useful in search word hunting
- information about average sentence length in the corpus material and the target text provided ideas about stylistic adequacy
- key word lists, in turn, were used for more targeted corpus text searches (described above). They were also used for stylistic purposes. In one case, the key word list made the group aware of the frequency of *you* and thus a preference for a more personal approach in English guide texts.

## 12.2 Software literacy

Most groups had, however, problems with the software and commented on their own lack of software literacy as well as inadequacies in the program. The main complaint was that *Wordsmith Tools* is not as simple as they were made to believe. There were some inconsistencies in the selectional procedures, many open windows caused problems and sometimes the system was incapable of coping with the multiple tasks it was asked to perform. For some impatient individuals, the learning threshold proved to be too high. The comments varied from no problems after a short initial period to major and frustrating problems. The on-line manual was criticized by a number of users and a trial-and-error method was widely applied instead of the manual.

# 13. Overall assessment of the benefits of disposable DIY corpora in translation

The main benefit of DIY corpora can be summarized as reassurance. When relevant corpus information was available, the users often gained reassurance for their strategic decisions as well as the actual lexical choices. They also found terms and other lexical expressions that could not have been found in dictionaries or glossaries.

Another general comment was that corpus evidence makes it easier for translators to make radical decisions. This evidence helps translators be less bound to the source material and feel much more confident when deviating from the way things are expressed in the source material if they feel that the changes are justified.

On the compilation side and the more technical side, the comments ranged from corpus design criteria to cost efficiency, the general role of

corpora and their cost efficiency. The groups came up with the following
types of recommendations:

- corpus design criteria need to be clear before compilation starts.
- finding relevant corpus material is often difficult. So a joint effort
  is needed, for example at the department, to compile special-field
  corpus collections[2]
- learning adequate search strategies is of crucial importance
- corpora should be used together with other reference sources, particularly dictionaries
- lack of software literacy can be a stumbling block
- in the end, it is the translator who is the decision-maker, not the
  corpus, which is never definitive

## 14. Lingering doubts

The compilers also came up with a number of doubts about their own
deductive strategies. For example:

- *Circularity.* Is there a danger of circularity when deciding on the
  key words in advance and then finding texts that use these key
  words to prove their applicability in a new context? On the other
  hand, if these key terms are widely used, this must mean that they
  are also current in the field. The conclusion was a recommendation
  to think carefully about the corpus design criteria.
- *Negative searches.* If a selected search term is non-existent or rare
  in the corpus, does it mean that it is also unsuitable for the translation? Is this a foolproof deduction? How much decisive power does
  a corpus carry? The conclusion was that corpora could not be trusted
  blindly. What is in them depends on the design criteria, available
  material and corpus size. Intuitive decisions should not be scrapped,
  but should be used together with corpus-based decisions.

---

[2] This comment seems to contradict the concept of disposability. Permanent collections could never be as precision-targeted as disposable ad hoc corpora. Yet, nothing
prevents disposable corpora from forming parts of more permanent collections that
have other uses in translation.

# 15. Conclusions and implications for the training of translators

If we accept the tenet that modern translational competence also includes corpus linguistic knowledge, then we need to think what this means in practice and what type of basic corpus skills should prospective translators be taught. On the basis of the present study, we can look at the skills needed in using disposable, virtual corpora to perform translation tasks. In a way, we are discussing the adaptation of an old practice to a modern electronic setting. To improve the quality of the end product, translators now have an immense comparable text resource available at their fingertips. The problem lies in finding the right material for any particular assignment.

In practical terms then, translator trainees need to be taught how to compile corpora, as well as how to use them in an intelligent way. If we try to sketch these skills as competencies, a tentative list could look like this:

Corpus compilation:
- corpus design and design criteria
- search strategies and search word selection
- source criticism to assess the reliability of corpus texts
- assessment of corpus adequacy and relevancy
- software literacy in general
- selection of internet search engines
- integrated use of word processing tools and corpus tools

Use of corpus information:
- deductive corpus analysis skills in general
- use of preliminary corpus information for more targeted compilation criteria
- use of corpus evidence for translational decisions
- corpus evaluation and decision-making skills
- distinctions between permanent corpus collections and targeted, disposable corpora
- overall corpus knowledge management skills

In addition, the curriculum could have an evaluative component to assess and promote the development of dedicated corpus software for translators. The focus in this part would thus be on the usability and user-friendliness of the existing software and its compatibility with other tools in the translator's workstation.

# References

Ahmad, Kurshid, Paul Holmes-Higgin and Syed Sibte Raza Abidi (1994) 'A Description of Texts in a Corpus: 'Virtual' and 'Real' Corpora', in Willy Martin, Willem Meijs, Margaret Moerland, Elsemiek ten Pas, Piet van Sterkenburg and Piet Vossen (eds) *EURALEX 1994 Proceedings*, Amsterdam: Vrije Universiteit, 390-402.

Carliner, Saul (1999) 'Knowledge Management, Intellectual Capital, and Technical Communication', in *Communication Jazz: Improvising the New International Communication Culture. Proceedings 1999 IEEE,* International Professional Communication Conference, New Orleans, September 1999, 85-91.

Lefevere, André (1992) *Translation, Rewriting and the Manipulation of Literary Fame*, London and New York: Routledge.

Scott, Mike (1996) *Wordsmith Tools*, Oxford: Oxford University Press.

Varantola, Krista (1994) 'The Dictionary User as Decision-maker', in Willy Martin, Willem Meijs, Margaret Moerland, Elsemiek ten Pas, Piet van Sterkenburg and Piet Vossen (eds) *EURALEX 1994 Proceedings*, Amsterdam: Vrije Universiteit, 606-611.

------ (2000) 'Translators, Dictionaries and Text Corpora', in Silvia Bernardini and Federico Zanettin (eds) *I corpora nella didattica della traduzione*, Bologna: CLUEB, 117-133.

Venuti, Laurence (1995) *The Translator's Invisibility*, London and New York: Routledge.

# Introducing *Compara*, the Portuguese-English Parallel Corpus

ANA FRANKENBERG-GARCIA AND DIANA SANTOS

*This paper is an introduction to the Portuguese-English parallel corpus, Compara. Compara is a machine-searchable and open-ended collection of Portuguese-English and English-Portuguese source texts and translations. It was made for people who have never used corpora before as well as for experienced corpus users. Compara's encoding and alignment criteria allow users to inspect translators' notes and investigate when and where translators have chosen to join, separate, delete, add and reorder sentences. Also, the corpus has been specifically designed to accommodate more than one translation per source text. Compara is freely accessible on the WWW.*

## 1. Introduction

Modelling itself on the core structure of the English-Norwegian Parallel Corpus (Johansson *et al.* 1999), *Compara* is a machine-readable and searchable collection of source texts originally written in Portuguese and in English that have been aligned with their respective English and Portuguese translations. For the present, *Compara* contains only published fiction, but other genres are expected to be added to the corpus at a later stage. *Compara* is encoded according to the IMS Corpus Workbench system, developed at the University of Stuttgart (Christ *et al.* 1999),[1] and can be searched online via the *Dispara* interface, which has been developed under the broader framework of the Computational Processing of Portuguese project.[2] *Compara* has been conceived for people who are not necessarily corpus-literate as well as for experienced corpus users, and should thus be useful for research purposes of varying complexity.

## 2. Corpus Structure

*Compara* is an open-ended corpus. This means that it can grow in whichever direction proves to become important to users, and that the texts

---

[1] For the IMS Corpus Workbench see: http://www.ims.uni-stuttgart.de/CorpusWorkbench/
[2] For further information on the Computational Processing of Portuguese project, see http://www.portugues.mct.pt

incorporated in the corpus can be put to use as soon as they are processed. Initially, *Compara* will not lend itself to studies that require large and representative language samples. However, as not all analyses depend on large corpora[3] and as there are no other publicly available corpora for the Portuguese-English language pair, it was felt that it was important to provide access to whatever was available as soon as it became available. An additional advantage of allowing users to access *Compara* at an early stage is that it is simpler to act on feedback from users when the corpus is small.

No a priori decisions were made regarding the kind of source texts and translations to be included in *Compara*, apart from the choice to limit the languages of the corpus to original English and English translated from Portuguese, and original Portuguese and Portuguese translated from English.[4] All varieties of Portuguese and English were considered, and no priority was given to any particular variety. The corpus was also structured so as to allow for the possibility of a source text being aligned with more than one translation.

Given this configuration, it is possible to use *Compara* to:

1. Study Portuguese translated from English and English translated from Portuguese.
2. Study Portuguese and English independently from one another.
3. Compare Portuguese and English source texts and translations from the six perspectives depicted in figure 1.[5]
4. Compare different translations of the same source text, as examples A and B illustrate (figures 2 and 3).

In example A, the source text can act as a common denominator for a study of similarities and differences between Brazilian and European Portuguese. In example B, the source text can act as a common denominator for a study of diachronic differences in translation.

A rather important corollary to this corpus structure is that conventional corpus design issues such as balance and representativeness are

---

[3] For Biber *et al.* (1998), different analyses require different sized corpora, and the optimum size of a corpus for an analysis to be reliable is something that can be investigated empirically. It has been shown that lexicographic studies, for example, require larger corpora than studies investigating grammar alone.
[4] Following Baker (1998), it is believed that there are distinctive differences between texts written originally in one language and texts translated into that same language.
[5] As in the English-Norwegian Parallel Corpus.

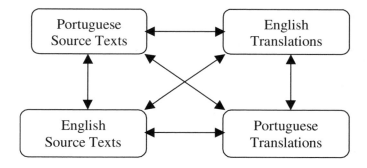

**Figure 1**. Structure of Compara

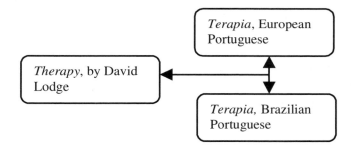

**Figure 2**. Example A

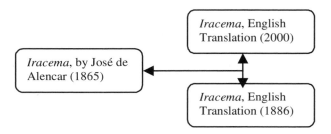

**Figure 3**. Example B

simply not addressed. The responsibility of achieving balance (if and when balance is an issue) and of judging the representativeness of the corpus for any given study is left in the hands of the user. To enable users to have control over this, it is possible for them to determine exactly which parts of *Compara* they wish to search. The corpus can be automatically narrowed down so as to search only within specific varieties of Portuguese and English, and any language variety combination is possible. For example, users can search only Brazilian Portuguese and British English, or all varieties of Portuguese but only American English, and so on. It is also possible to narrow down the corpus by date of publication. Users who wish to focus only on contemporary (or non-contemporary) language, for example, can automatically remove from their searches source texts and translations published before (or after) any particular date. The third narrowing-down option available allows users to select exactly which texts they want to use in their searches, thus creating their own, tailor-made sub-corpora of *Compara*. For example, it is possible to search texts by only one particular author, group of authors, translator, and so on.

Eventually, when texts of different genres are included in the corpus, there will also be an option that allows users to select texts automatically by genre. To help users assess the questions of balance and representativeness, access to information on the size of each separate text in the corpus is provided. The full reference of all the texts in the corpus plus extra-textual information on copyright and language variety are also provided.

## 3.  Text selection

Although *Compara* is to remain open to different genres, the initial corpus contains only fiction. Obtaining copyright clearance for a corpus of fiction is notoriously difficult, and requesting permission to use the same texts in two different languages is twice as complicated. For the Portuguese-English language pair, however, there are several good reasons for taking fiction as a starting point.

To understand this, one should note that in the world there is far more English translated into Portuguese than Portuguese translated into English. When looking at how this reality applies to a few individual genres, it can be seen that:

- *Academic prose.* There are practically no translations of Portuguese into English. Portuguese-speaking intellectuals and scientists usually

write and publish directly in either Portuguese or English, and it is
only very rarely that academic books and articles originally written
in Portuguese appear in English translation. Conversely, as most
Portuguese-speaking academics are expected to be able to read in
English, scientific articles in English translated into Portuguese are
not very common.

- *Journalistic texts.* Although Portuguese-language magazines and
newspapers often buy news articles written in English, the Portuguese version they publish is often an adaptation more than a
translation.[6] Conversely, Portuguese-language newspaper articles
in English translation are practically non-existent.

- *Instruction booklets.* There is far more English translated into Portuguese than Portuguese translated into English in the texts that
accompany consumer goods. Also, these texts do not usually go
through the editing and proofreading stages normally required of
published texts,[7] so their quality can be extremely variable. Finally,
it is not always possible to determine whether Portuguese has been
translated directly from English and English from Portuguese: this
type of translation is often relayed, with other languages standing
in between.

- *Tourist brochures.* Tourist brochures in Portuguese translation
are practically non-existent: Portuguese-speaking tourists abroad
are expected to get by in other, more widely known languages.
In contrast, almost all material destined to be read by tourists in
Portuguese-speaking countries comes with an English translation.
Quality is also an issue. Like instruction booklets, tourist brochures
do not seem to be as carefully edited and proofread as published
texts.

- *Fiction.* Although the amount of Portuguese fiction translated into
English cannot be compared with the amount of English fiction in
Portuguese translation, there are quite a few Portuguese-speaking
fiction writers who have been translated into English.[8] A survey

---

[6] R.Garcia, journalist at the Portuguese daily *Publico*, personal communication. Pearson
(this volume) reaches similar conclusions after analysing French translations of *Scientific American.*

[7] For Biber (1993), 'published' means not only printed in multiple copies, but also
copyright registered or recorded by a major indexing service.

[8] Similarly, there is more English fiction translated into Norwegian than Norwegian
fiction translated into English (Johansson *et al.* 1999).

carried out at the very beginning of this project revealed that there are over 100 titles currently in print. Although there is no absolute guarantee of quality in the translation of fiction, these translations usually have to go through several stages of editing and proofreading, and are normally undertaken by qualified and experienced translators, not to mention the fact that the quality of the source texts is also relevant – while original fiction has to merit publication in the first place, this is not always true of certain tourist brochures, instruction manuals, etc.

This is obviously not the place for an extensive analysis of the present Portuguese-English translation reality for each individual genre. The brief outline given above, however, should serve to justify the choice for an initial corpus of fiction.

As *Compara* is publicly accessible on the Internet, we anticipated that it would be extremely hard to obtain permission to use fiction texts that are still in copyright. This factor overruled all possible arguments in favour of requesting permission to use whole texts.[9] Despite the choice to use extracts rather than entire texts, an attempt was made not to replicate design problems encountered in other corpora based on text extracts. The English-Norwegian Parallel Corpus, for example, used similar length extracts taken only from the beginnings of novels, and this was found to be a disadvantage by Santos and Oksefjell (1999) when attempting to validate corpus-based contrastive work. In *Compara*, extracts of around 30% of the total of each work were selected at random from their beginning, middle or end.

## 4.  Alignment

Aligning source texts and translations is not simple, for translators do not always translate texts in a predictable and linear manner. Translators may (and often do):

- split source-text sentences into two or more sentences in the translation
- join two or more source-text sentences together, rendering them as a single translation sentence

---

[9] See Baker (1995), for example.

- leave things out
- insert elements that were not present in the source text
- reorder elements so that the order in which they appear in the translation differs from that in which they appear in the source text.

Existing parallel corpora which take the sentence as the basic unit for text alignment assume that sentences are not very often split, joined and reordered in translation (Véronis, 2000). They also do not pay too much heed to the direction of translation. Although these assumptions might be necessary if one is to automatically align large amounts of text, they also prevent one from using aligned corpora to study factors which are in themselves interesting to translation studies: i.e., what makes translators join, separate, add, remove or reorder sentences.

In *Compara*, we felt it was important to align texts directionally always from source to translation. This would not only open the way to a better understanding of translators' decisions, but would also facilitate the process of analysing multiple translations of the same source text. The basic unit of alignment in *Compara* was therefore defined as the source-text sentence, which means the direction of translation is intrinsically taken into account.

Whenever there is not a one-to-one sentence correspondence between source and translation, the sentences in the translation are split or joined together to conform to the way sentences were originally divided in the source text. Thus an alignment unit is always one orthographic sentence in the source text and the corresponding text in the translation, whether it is one, more than one, or even only part of a sentence. Source-text sentences that have been left out of the translation are aligned with blank units. Sentences that have been added to the translation with no corresponding text in the original are fitted into the nearest preceding alignment unit. Figure 4 summarizes these alignment criteria.

Apart from the above, if there are any sentences that have been reordered in the translation, they are aligned with the sentences that prompted them in the source texts, and the original published order is marked so that sentence reordering, a non-trivial aspect of translation studies, can be automatically retrieved. None of the existing automatic aligners seem to take the direction of translation into account.

The aligner used in *Compara* – EasyAlign tool (v.1.0) written for use with the IMS Corpus Workbench – does not single out source text sentence divisions as being more important than translation text divisions.

| SOURCE | | TRANSLATION |
|--------|---|-------------|
| S | → | S |
| S | → | S,S |
| S | → | ½ S |
| S | → | ∅ |
| S | → | S(+S) |

**Figure 4**. Alignment criteria

Whenever source and translation sentence divisions do not correspond, EasyAlign either matches one (source sentence) to many (translation sentences) – which is fine according to *Compara*'s alignment criteria – or it matches many (source sentences) to one (translation sentence) – which is not what *Compara*'s alignment requires. When one-to-many cases occur, automatic sentence separators for Portuguese and English are applied in order to tag those translation units appropriately. When many-to-one matches are detected, the source text sentences that have been kept together have to be manually separated and matched to the corresponding text in the translation.

Because *Compara*'s alignment criteria require that source-texts should always be divided in the same way no matter which translation they are aligned with, source texts can act as common denominators to multiple translations, as previously shown in figure 2. Also, because the alignment is directional, it is possible to search automatically for translational discourse changes such as when and where translators have decided to join, split, delete, add or reorder sentences.[10]

---

[10] Ideally, it would have been desirable to retrieve the addition, deletion and reordering of clauses, for, as Malmkjær (1997) put it, it is at the level of the clause that translation sense for sense and translation structure for structure usually meet. Empirical evidence of this for the Portuguese-English pair can be found in Santos (1994). Clause alignment was not an option, however, because of the extreme difficulty in detecting clause boundaries automatically.

# 5. Additional markup

Apart from alignment markup, *Compara* also marks highlighted text whenever it is used to set off titles, foreign words or within-sentence emphasis, thus facilitating the automatic retrieval of these features. Categorizing highlighted text in this way, however, is not as straightforward and unambiguous as it seems. In Julian Barnes's *Flaubert's Parrot*, for example, titles like *Un coeur simple* and *Madame Bovary* can be classified as both title and foreign. However, in the case of *Madame Bovary,* since both the English and Portuguese translations of this title are also *Madame Bovary,* and given that *Madame Bovary* is a proper name, it could be reasonably argued that it should be marked just title, but not foreign.

Marking foreign words *per se* is also not simple. The boundaries dividing what an author or translator (not to mention a corpus maker) considers or not to be foreign is by no means clear-cut. For example, in Margaret Jull Costa's English translation of Sá-Carneiro's *Lúcio's Confession,* words like *coupé* and *décolletage* are not in italics but *manqué* and *passé* are. There may also be a certain amount of difficulty in discriminating between text that has been highlighted because it is foreign and text that has been highlighted for emphasis. In David Lodge's *Therapy,* at one point it is hard to tell whether *Au contraire* has been italicised just because it is foreign or both because it is foreign and for emphasis.

For the sake of consistency, then, the criteria outlined in figure 5 have been adopted when inserting title, foreign and emphasis marks. According to these criteria:

a. Titles and foreign and emphatic words and phrases that have not been highlighted by the author or the translator have not been marked in the corpus.

b. Highlighted text indicating features other than titles, foreign words and phrases, and within-sentence emphasis (like changes of voice, for example) have not been marked.

c. Whenever the categories for title, foreign and emphasis overlap, title overrules foreign, which in turn overrules emphasis. Thus emphasis is only marked if it is neither foreign nor title, and foreign is only marked if it is not title.

In addition to the above, translators' notes have also been marked and have been inserted in the text at the point which their identifiers appear.

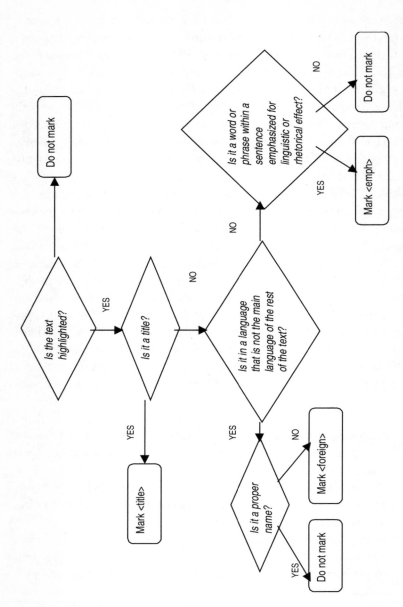

**Figure 5.** Criteria adopted when inserting title, foreign and emphasis marks

This allows users to study exactly when, where and why translators' notes were thought to be appropriate. The implementation of this particular feature involved the initial removal of the notes in order not to damage automatic alignment, and then putting them automatically back in place.

Obvious typographical errors that escaped proofreading in the editions from which the texts were extracted have been corrected and marked. However, because we assumed that the retrieval of these errors was not important for translation studies, there is no corresponding query in the interface.

# 6. Accessibility

One of our major concerns in creating *Compara* was to make it widely accessible to anyone interested in comparing and contrasting English and Portuguese. The most logical way of providing widespread access to *Compara* seemed to be to enable the corpus to be searched via the Internet.[11] A particularly delicate matter for a corpus that is to be made available online is the copyright issue. In *Compara*, users only have access to the results of their search queries, and are not be able to read or copy the corpus excerpts in their entirety.[12] The groundwork for actually making *Compara* available online had been previously laid by the *Computational Processing of Portuguese* project, whose objective is to create, evaluate, catalogue and distribute Portuguese language computational resources. Thanks to their collaboration, providing free online access to *Compara* was mainly a matter of developing the *Dispara* interface, which serves as a bridge between the *IMS Corpus Workbench* software and the specific requirements of *Compara*.

*Compara* can be accessed free of charge at http://www.portugues.mct.pt/ *Compara*/. No registering or password is necessary. Every page in the *Compara* website is available in both Portuguese and English, so that people with very little Portuguese or very little English can still access

---

[11] Several other advantages of making corpora available online are outlined in Santos (1998).

[12] The maximum number of concordances shown is 500. If the user chooses to search only a subset of the corpus, then this number is further limited to 200. Whenever the results exceed these limits, the concordances shown are selected at random. Even if for certain queries it is not possible to *show* all the concordances, the total number of solutions found is always provided, so that the user can at least have a quantitative measure of the results.

them. Two search options are available. The *Simple Search* was made for people who have never used corpora before. It allows users to search the entire corpus either in the Portuguese-English or in the English-Portuguese direction. The *Complex Search* was made for those who want to conduct more sophisticated queries. It allows users to choose the search direction (an option to consider if the directionality of translation is relevant to a particular query), to narrow down the corpus (and so control which texts they are going to use if their queries require a balanced corpus or a specific subset or other of the corpus), and to select how the results are to be presented. Users can view concordances, distribution of forms (for queries involving more than one form, for example, *untrue/false*), distribution of sources (how a search expression is distributed in the texts within the corpus) and a quantitative wrap up (the distribution of the search expression in the two languages, for searches that involve alignment constraints – see below). When defining a query, the *IMS Corpus Workbench* syntax (Christ *et al.* 1999) can be used to include in a single query different spellings of a word (for example, *analyse* and *analyze*), different morphological variants of a word (for example, *walk*, *walked*, *walks*, etc.), a word and a collocate with any number of elements in between (for example *make* and *decision*), and so on. It is also possible to enter alignment constraints. For example, users searching for the Portuguese translation of *yes*, which is often rendered as *sim*, can retrieve just the cases in which *yes* is translated into *sim* or just the cases in which *yes* is translated into something other than *sim*.[13]

In addition to this, users can inspect translators' notes, emphasis, foreign words and expressions, and titles. Finally, users can inspect alignment properties and see when and where translators have decided to join, separate, delete and add sentences to the translation. The possibility of looking at reordered sentences was not yet operational at the time this paper was written.

## 7.  Output

Thinking of language learning and translation training in particular, it was important that the results should be presented in a way that would be

---

[13] There is no underlying word alignment. The search is based on finding out whether or not *sim* is present in the Portuguese alignment unit corresponding to the English alignment unit containing *yes*.

easily transposable to the classroom. The concordances in *Compara* are displayed in two columns, with the Portuguese or English search item appearing in bold on the left-hand side, and the corresponding text in English or Portuguese on the right-hand side. Displaying the results in columns rather than in rows makes it easier for the user to compare different translations of the same search string and scroll up and down the results on screen.

Instead of a key-word-in-context (KWIC) concordance with a fixed number of characters to the left and to the right, the context is always one full source-text sentence and the corresponding text in the translation. Full source text sentences can help one understand the choices underlying a given translation better than a set number of characters to the left and to the right of the search string, although in some cases more co-text may be necessary. There are plans to allow the user to expand the amount of co-text given within the limits of fair-use, but this feature was not yet operational at the time this paper was written. Next to each parallel concordance displayed, there is a link to the full reference of the pair of texts from where it was retrieved. This makes it easier for users to identify the source text and the translation in question, should additional, extra-textual information (like authorship, date of publication, language variety, and so on) be important to help one understand a translation.

Language learners can be trained to use *Compara* to look things up for themselves, and there are many ways the corpus can be used in the language or translation classroom. As proposed in Frankenberg-Garcia (2000, 2002), it is not unduly complicated to edit the results obtained in *Compara* so as to convert them into teaching materials. Appendix 1 contains a sample cloze exercise based on the output of *Compara*, in which students are required to give the Portuguese translation of *even,* a word liable to create confusion among native speakers of Portuguese given its different meanings and translations. To prepare the exercise, a search for *even* was carried out in *Compara*, and the results were saved as an HTML file. The file was then opened from within a word processor and edited. The table menu was used to delete the row where corpus reference links appear (not necessary for the exercise), and the replace function was used to change the Portuguese translations of *even* (*até, mesmo, sequer* and *ainda*) into blank spaces.

Appendix 2 contains an extract of a worksheet prepared to help students understand different uses of negative prefixes in English and Portuguese. Based on the principle of data-driven learning (Johns 1991), students are asked to look at the concordances extracted from *Compara* and underline the Portuguese words that correspond to English words beginning with the negative prefix *un*. The exercise helps students realize that negative prefixes seem to be used much more sparingly in Portuguese, and that translators use different strategies to deal with them. Out of the 57 occurences of English words beginning with the negative prefix *un* contained in the total exercise, less than half were translated into a word containing a Portuguese negative prefix. Negative particles and root antonyms (for example, *false* instead of *untrue*) were frequently used as alternative translation strategies.

## 8.  Current corpus and concluding remarks

*Compara* was first announced in January 2001. At the time this paper was written, *Compara* had permission to include extracts of 60 different Portuguese-English text-pairs by authors and translators from Angola, Brazil, Mozambique, Portugal, South Africa, the United Kingdom and the United States. These texts represent the combined product of the work of 33 authors and 31 translators.[14] The part of the corpus available for research presently adds up to around 190 K words in each language. In less than six months, *Compara* has had over 3000 visits from more than 400 different computers. It is hoped that feedback from users will contribute towards the development of *Compara*, and that this might take place alongside a growing interest in the use of corpora for research and education.

## References

Baker, Mona (1995) 'Corpora in Translation Studies: An Overview and Some Suggestions for Future Research', *Target* 7(2): 223-243.
------ (1998) 'Réexplorer la Langue de la Traduction: Une Approche par Corpus', *Meta* 43(4): 480-485.
Biber, Douglas (1993) 'Representativeness in Corpus Design', *Literary and Linguistic Computing* 8: 243-257.
------, Susan Conrad and Rendi Reppen (1998) *Corpus Linguistics: Investigating Language Structure And Use,* Cambridge: Cambridge University Press.

---

[14] For a full, regularly updated list of the texts in COMPARA, see: http://www.portugues.mct.pt/COMPARA/CorpusContents.html

Christ, Oliver, Bruno M. Schulze, Anja Hofmann and Esther Koenig (1999) *The IMS Corpus Workbench: Corpus Query Processor (CQP): User's Manual,* Institute for Natural Language Processing, University of Stuttgart, March 8, 1999 (CQP V2.2), online: http://www.ims.unistuttgart.de/projekte/CorpusWorkbench/CQPUserManual/HTML/

Frankenberg-Garcia, Ana (2000) 'Using a Translation Corpus to Teach English to Native Speakers of Portuguese', *Op.Cit.* 3: 65-78.

------ (2002) 'Compara, Language Learning and Translation Training', in Belinda Maia, Johann Haller and Margherita Ulrych (eds) *Training the Language Services Provider for the New Millennium,* Porto: Faculdade de Letras da Universidade do Porto, 187-198.

Johansson, Stig, Jarle Ebeling and Signe Oksefjell (1999) *English-Norwegian Parallel Corpus: Manual,* online: http://www.hf.uio.no/iba/prosjekt/ENPCmanual.html

Johns, Tim (1991) 'Should You Be Persuaded: Two Examples of Data-driven Learning Materials', *ELR Journal* 4: 1-16.

Malmkjær, Kirsten (1997) 'Unit of Translation' in Mona Baker (ed) *The Routledge Encyclopedia of Translation Studies,* New York and London: Routledge, 286-288.

Santos, Diana (1994) 'Bilingual Alignment and Tense' in *Proceedings of the Second Annual Workshop on Very Large Corpora* (Kyoto, 4 August 1994), ACL, 129-141.

------ (1998) 'Providing Access to Language Resources through the World Wide Web: The Oslo Corpus of Bosnian Texts', in Antonio Rubio, Natividad Gallardo, Rosa Castro and Antonio Tejada (eds) *Proceedings of The First International Conference on Language Resources and Evaluation* (Granada, 28-30 May 1998), 1: 475-481.

------ and Signe Oksefjell (1999) 'Using a Parallel Corpus to Validate Independent Claims', *Languages in Contrast* 2(1): 117-132.

Véronis, Jean (ed) (2000) *Parallel Text Processing,* Dordrecht: Kluwer Academic Publishers.

## Appendix 1

Exercise based on output of *Compara http://www.portugues.mct.pt/ Compara/ [15-May-2001]*

## Fill in the gaps with an appropriate Portuguese translation for *even*:

| | |
|---|---|
| I had the ideas; I **even** made notes. | Tinha as ideias; _____ coligi notas. |
| They had planned the trip in detail, had their hair specially curled for the occasion, and had **even** stolen flowers for the girls. | Tinham planeado a visita em pormenor, tinham ondulado especialmente o cabelo para a ocasião, e _____ tinham roubado flores para as raparigas. |
| Memories came out of hiding, but not emotions; not **even** the memories of emotions. | Surgiam as recordações, mas não as emoções; nem _____ recordações de emoções. |
| The other rooms contained medical instruments of the eighteenth and nineteenth centuries: heavy metal relics coming to sharp points, and enema pumps of a calibre which surprised **even** me. | As outras salas tinham instrumentos médicos dos séculos XVIII e XIX: pesadas relíquias de metal que terminavam em pontas agudas e irrigadores de um calibre que _____ a mim me surpreendia. |
| She keeps the adored relic beside her, and **even** takes to saying her prayers while kneeling before him. | Guarda junto de si a relíquia adorada e começa _____ a dizer as suas orações ajoelhada na sua frente. |
| A cheeky bird, inducing affection, **even** reverence. | Um pássaro atrevido, que suscitava afecto, respeito _____. |
| All that remains of Flaubert's residence is a small one-storey pavilion a few hundred yards down the road: a summer house to which the writer would retire when needing **even** more solitude than usual. | Tudo o que ficou da residência de Flaubert é um pequeno pavilhão a poucas centenas de metros da estrada: uma casa de Verão para onde o autor se retirava quando precisava de _____ maior solidão do que a habitual. |
| Then I realised the fallacy in this: Flaubert, after all, hadn't been given a choice of parrots; and **even** this second one, which looked the calmer company, might well get on your nerves after a couple of weeks. | Depois descobri a ironia disto: Flaubert, apesar de tudo, não tinha podido escolher o papagaio; e _____ o segundo, que parecia uma companhia mais calma, podia muito bem tornar-se irritante depois de umas semanas. |

## *Appendix 2*
Exercise based on output of *Compara* http://www.portugues.mct.pt/ *Compara/* [10-May-2001]

### Read the extracts below and underline the Portuguese word or words that correspond to English words beginning with the negative prefix *un*:

| | |
|---|---|
| The thrower remained a stylish, temporary statue: knees not quite **unbent**, and the right hand ecstatically spread. | O jogador ficou como uma estilizada estátua temporária: os joelhos um pouco dobrados e a mão direita erguida e estática. |
| Let me start with the statue: the one above, the permanent, **unstylish** one, the one crying cupreous tears, the floppy-tied, square waistcoated, baggy-trousered, straggle-moustached, wary, aloof bequeathed image of the man. | Vou começar pela estátua: a de cima, a permanente, a sem estilo, a que chora lágrimas de cobre, a que lega à posteridade a imagem circunspecta de um homem com um laço desajeitado, colete quadrado, calças largas como sacos, bigode em desalinho. |
| If so, then how tantalising are the **unfinished** books. | Se assim é, então que excitantes são os livros inacabados. |
| The **unwritten** books? | Os livros que não se escreveram? |
| Dot, dash, dash, dash went: the concrete caissons, with the **unhurried** water between them. | Ponto, traço, traço, traço, faziam as caixas de cimento, separadas umas das outras pela água calma. |
| I was close to where friends had died - the sudden friends those years produced - and yet I felt **unmoved**. | Ali perto amigos meus tinham morrido - os amigos inesperados que esses anos nos dão - mas não me sentia comovido. |
| But here, in this **unexceptional** green parrot, preserved in a routine yet mysterious fashion, was something which made me feel I had almost known the writer. | Mas aqui, neste vulgar papagaio verde, perservado de uma maneira vulgar e no entanto misteriosa, havia algo que me fazia sentir que quase tinha conhecido o escritor. |
| It's about a poor, **uneducated** servant-woman called Félicité, who serves the same mistress for half a century, unresentfully sacrificing her own life to those of others. | É acerca de uma pobre criada ignorante chamada Félicité, que serve a mesma patroa durante meio século, sacrificando sem ressentimentos a sua vida à dos outros. |

# Corpora, Translation and Multilingual Computing

TONY MCENERY AND PAUL BAKER

*In this paper we survey current development in the provision of corpus data for use in the research and practice of translation. While conceding that much research and development for indigenous European languages is needed, we argue that non-indigenous minority languages in Europe are both an important source of domestic translation tasks and are poorly served with corpora/language processing tools.*

## 1. Introduction

McEnery and Wilson (1994) provided an overview and made some predictions about the use of corpora in translation studies. Multilingual corpora have developed greatly over the past decade and in this paper we will re-explore the prospects for corpora and translation. In doing so, we will be reporting in part on research undertaken as part of the Minority Language Engineering (MILLE)[1] project, which reviewed the provision of basic language processing materials for a wide range of UK non-indigenous minority languages. However, before turning to that project and its findings regarding corpora and translation, it seems appropriate to return to the predictions made in 1994.

## 2. What has happened to corpora and translation since 1994?

The general thrust of the 1994 paper was that more corpora were needed in European languages, annotated in a variety of ways, to be of use in translation studies. Since that time, many resources have been made available for European languages – the *CRATER* project (McEnery *et al.* 1997) has provided 1,000,000 word parallel corpora of English, French and Spanish, *MULTEXT* (Véronis and Khouri 1995) has created monolingual and parallel corpora for all of the official languages of the EU[2], and *MULTEXT*

---

[1] Funded by the UK EPSRC, project reference GR/L96400.
[2] See http://www.uic.edu/orgs/tei/app/mu03.html for details.

*East* (Erjavec *et al.* 1995) has provided similar data for a wide range of East European languages.[3] Additionally, projects such as *PAROLE* undertook to create monolingual resources for the official languages of the EU.[4]

As corpora have become more widely available, so corpus annotation has spread across a wide range of languages. While ten years ago syntactically annotated corpora (so-called 'treebanks') were rare and confined largely to English, they are now available for numerous languages. For example, on the *Verbmobil project*, treebanks of English, German and Japanese were developed with the specific aim of constructing a speech-to-speech automated translation (see, for example, Kordoni 2000 and Stegmann *et al.* 1998).[5] Such an example shows how corpus annotation has been made multilingual in the past decade and how it is being applied directly to translation related issues.

With an ever-growing number of projects focusing on the provision of monolingual and parallel corpora for European languages, the need outlined in the 1994 paper for an increase in the provision of corpora to enable corpus based approaches to the study and practice of translation seems to have been met to some degree. This is not to say that any conceivable corpus for any conceivable purpose is now available for European languages. Indeed, while the volumes of data provided by projects such as *CRATER* appear impressive, the scope of the data often proves to be disappointing – *CRATER* only includes technical manuals, for example. Indeed genre seems to be the major limiting factor at the moment, at least in terms of what parallel material is available. While parallel corpora of technical manuals (*CRATER*), European parliamentary proceedings (*MULTEXT*) and translations of Plato (*MULTEXT East*) are undoubtedly of use to some researchers, they are still not ideal representations of the full range of material which is translated between the languages of the EU. So while the development of parallel and monolingual corpora in the 1990s must be welcomed, it is still to be lamented that the corpora developed were often very narrow in terms of the range of genres represented within them.

Nonetheless, it is undoubtedly the case that researchers wishing to take a corpus based approach to the study and practice of translation for Euro-

---

[3] See http://www.uic.edu/orgs/tei/app/mu04.html for details.
[4] See http://www.icp.inpg.fr/ELRA/cata/doc/parole.html for details.
[5] See http://verbmobil.dfki.de/cgi-bin/verbmobil/htbin/doc-access.cgi for a full listing of research reports for this project.

pean languages are in a much better position now than they were in the early 1990s. It is noteworthy, however, that the major parallel corpus building projects have been EU funded, and have focused expressly upon indigenous European languages. It was in part in response to that focus that the *MILLE* project was established in the UK to focus on issues concerning research into and translation of non-indigenous minority languages.

## 3. The MILLE Project

As demonstrated in the previous section, the number of corpora available for the study of indigenous European languages has improved enormously over the past decade. However, it should be noted that indigenous European languages, while the focus perhaps of international translation in Europe, are rarely the main target for domestic translation across the EU. A good example of this is the UK. While UK companies exporting to mainland Europe do have a need to translate materials into the official languages of the European Union, the translation needs occurring within the UK are entirely different. A large amount of translation aimed at a national audience takes place in the UK, for example the Department of Social Security, Department of Health and local councils all regularly translate advice leaflets. However, little of this translation occurs with respect to indigenous European languages. The obvious exceptions are indigenous minority languages, such as Welsh. However, for most local councils and government departments, the languages important for domestic translation tasks are, in alphabetical order: Arabic, Bengali, Chinese, Gujarati, Hindi, Panjabi, Polish, Somali, Turkish and Urdu. Consequently, an important issue arises – if corpora are of potential benefit to the study and practice of translation, then what corpus resources are available for languages important for domestic as opposed to international translation purposes? Initial findings from the *MILLE* project (McEnery *et al.* 2000) indicated that a great deal of work was needed to bring some of these languages, especially South Asian languages, to the same level of provision of corpus data as indigenous European languages.

One argument that may be put forward by European researchers is that this is more a question for South Asia than the UK. However, such a response would miss two important points. Firstly, corpus linguistics is nowhere near as well developed in South Asia, and currently there is no prospect of the situation improving in the near future (ibid.). Secondly, and importantly for translation studies, even if corpora of South Asian languages were available from India and other countries of the sub-continent, these would be of marginal use for translators in the UK context. Much translation of South Asian languages in the UK context is of highly specialised, term rich texts which are very specific to the UK context, such as leaflets outlining entitlements to social security benefits. The task of producing non-indigenous minority language data, especially parallel corpus data, is rightly that of the countries in which those languages are being translated. While some assistance from countries where these are majority or official languages may be expected, the provision of such assistance is neither a necessary prerequisite for the development of such resources, nor sufficient in itself to meet the needs of those translating these documents in a different cultural context.

To support the argument that it was in the area of domestic translation, rather than international translation focused on Europe, that urgent research activity was required we decided to review what was translated in the UK. In doing so, we were also interested in discovering whether the relative under-provision of corpus data for South Asian languages had any direct impact upon the provision of translation aids for translators working in those languages.

## 4.   The translation process in the UK

In order to review the domestic translation market in the UK we conducted a survey of translation agencies and individual translators in the UK. In doing so we were greatly aided by the *Association of Translation Companies* in the UK, who identified a number of typical translation agencies in the UK regularly engaged in domestic translation tasks who were willing to participate in our study. Within translation agencies, individual translators responded to our survey. Each respondent was sent a 29-item questionnaire (see Appendix 1).

The translation agencies involved in the survey were *New Words* (Newcastle), *Sunderland Social Services, Department of Interpreting and Translation Services, Sakura Communications Feling, Materials Division* (University of Newcastle upon Tyne), *K International* (Milton Keynes) and *Language Line* (London). We received 24 completed questionnaires in total. The amount of experience possessed by each translator varied, with some being relatively new to the job, while others having worked as translators for a decade or more (see Table 1).

| Experience (years) | Number |
|---|:---:|
| less than 1 | 2 |
| 1-5 | 9 |
| 6-10 | 7 |
| 11-20 | 5 |
| 21+ | 1 |

**Table 1.** Length of experience of translators

In addition to this practical experience, we also found that the translators were on the whole well qualified. Although eight subjects had received no formal training, three had received Bachelors degrees in languages, one an MA, seven were DSPI qualified, two had degrees in translation and three had carried out training courses leading to certificates in translation.

The languages the subjects specialised in are summarised below (some translators specialised in more than one language). Table 2 largely supports the argument presented in section three – the translators were typically

| Language | Number |
|---|:---:|
| Urdu | 5 |
| Chinese | 4 |
| Hindi | 3 |
| Arabic | 2 |
| Bengali | 2 |
| French | 2 |
| German | 2 |
| Panjabi | 2 |
| Spanish | 2 |
| Danish | 1 |
| Hebrew | 1 |
| Japanese | 1 |
| Swedish | 1 |
| Tamil | 1 |

**Table 2.** Languages worked with by translators

not translating into indigenous European languages.

Considering the rather uneven provision of parallel corpus data we also decided to survey what types of documents these agencies translated. While some of the genres covered by current parallel corpora were represented in the responses, other document types presented in Table 3, notably marriage/birth/death certificates have never been the subject of parallel corpus construction.

| Type of document | Number |
|---|---|
| health-related documents | 12 |
| policy documents | 9 |
| marriage/birth/death certificates | 7 |
| social services | 6 |
| legal documents | 5 |
| police documents | 5 |
| technical/instruction manuals | 5 |
| news/magazine articles | 3 |
| educational documents | 3 |
| letters | 2 |
| election documents | 2 |
| annual reports | 2 |

**Table 3.** Genre of documents translated

## 4.1   Computational Resources Used

The survey revealed that domestic translation in the UK occurred in a range of non-indigenous languages, with South Asian languages being particularly important. The translation covered a range of genres. Typically, the languages and genres being translated in the survey are ones for which no parallel – or even monolingual – corpus data is available. Given that corpus data has been used for European languages to improve translation aids from dictionaries to MT systems, we were interested in examining how translation in corpus-poor languages was approached. As part of this the translators were asked to report if they used a variety of computational tools in their work - the results are shown in Table 4.

| Type of Tool | Language | Number |
|---|---|---|
| Printed Dictionaries | Bilingual | 23 |
| | Monolingual English | 18 |
| | Monolingual other languages | 13 |
| Word Processors | English | 20 |
| | Other languages | 18 |
| Spell-checkers | English | 17 |
| | Other languages | 7 |
| Online dictionaries | English | 5 |
| | Other languages | 3 |
| Other tools | English | 4 |
| | Other languages | 5 |

**Table 4.** Tools used to aid translation

In surveying this list, the most obvious finding is quite unsurprising – English tools are more widely used than tools for other languages, purely because of their availability. Yet while word-processing is used for languages other than English, there is a disparate range of word-processors used for processing non-English texts. The most frequently mentioned English word processor used was Microsoft Word (14 respondents), although other word processors were also used (Claris Works, WordPerfect, Quark Express). However, with respect to word processors working on non-Roman writing systems there was a much wider range of responses given; a variety of word processors were used (Al-Nashir, Page Composure, Microsoft Word Arabic, Twinbridge, Span Word 6, German Word 97, NisusWriter Hebrew, Bhoopalam, Access, Unitype). As each of these packages needs to be purchased and its interface learnt, it is clear that there is a higher financial and training overhead at present for those wishing to word-process in non-Roman writing systems.

As part of exploring whether computational resources based on corpus data was lacking for the non-European languages in question, we asked the subjects if they were satisfied with the amount of English language computational resources available for translation. Of the eighteen who replied, fifteen said yes, one said they were adequate and two said they could be better. However, when we asked the same question for foreign language computational resources, only nine of the seventeen people who answered said yes. Two said they were OK but could be better and six were dissatisfied. Of those who were not satisfied, four were working with right-to-left languages (Urdu and Arabic); two were working with Chinese and two with other Indian languages (Panjabi and Tamil). The two Urdu translators stressed that information technology for Urdu needed much more development. The Hebrew translator commented on the lack of termbanks for Hebrew. Additionally, a couple of the translators noted that the foreign language software that they used was unstable or unreliable.

We also asked whether the respondents found information technology useful in their translation work. Four people had never used it (translators of Hindi, Urdu, Panjabi/Urdu and Chinese), eighteen said it was very useful, one said not really and one said it had advantages and disadvantages (it helped finding words, but could result in the text being over-simplified). Several respondents noted that in order to produce translation work of high quality there was no option but to use computational tools. Others stressed the efficiency, reliability and speed of electronic resources in aiding the translation task. Dictionaries and spell-checkers were also viewed as particularly helpful.

The situation seems to be that translators are aware of the usefulness of computational tools, and feel that the languages they are processing compare very unfavourably to English in terms of computational support. Specifically, many of the resources requested – dictionaries, spell checkers and termbanks – are typically resources where corpora have an important role to play in the development stage.

In summary, while electronic translation tools have revolutionised the way that translators approach their work during the past decade, greater advances have been made for English than for UK non-indigenous languages. While the translation may initially be hand-written, the finished project is usually word-processed. Although the majority of the respondents were happy with resources provided for English word-processing, only about half were satisfied with resources in languages other than English.

## 4.2    Applications and tools

It appears to be the case then, that a large number of translators are working on languages where it is not possible to undertake a corpus based approach to translation research and practice – the corpora are not available. As a consequence of this many of the resources translators may expect to use, which in turn are based on corpora, are not available for these languages (e.g. termbanks) or are available but are not corpus based (e.g. dictionaries). However, just because the corpora are created we cannot assume that researchers will automatically want to work on these languages. Consequently, in a separate survey with 57 respondents (partly reported in McEnery *et al.* 2000) we asked linguists and language engineers to imagine that they had a cd of corpus data for a range of European non-indigenous minority languages in both written and spoken formats. We then asked them what sort of questions they would want to explore with such a corpus.

Encouragingly for the findings of our survey of translators, the most common answers for linguists were questions involving: machine translation (9), dictionary and vocabulary building (7), teaching aids (6), speech recognition (3), text-to-speech (2), spell-checkers (3), computational grammars (2) and information retrieval (2). For language engineers, the most common answers involved: semantics (7), language contact issues (loanwords, dialect, code-switching) (6), syntax (4), differences in genre/contexts (4), phonology (4), frequencies (3), dictionary and vocabulary building (2), interpersonal/discourse (2) and prosody (2).

In both lists, the types of tools and resources which translators currently working on non-indigenous minority languages lack are present – dictionary building, machine translation systems and spell-checkers. However, it is one thing for a researcher to say what they would do in a perfect world and quite another for them to decide to commit precious research time to exploring a new area. Consequently, we asked the respondents to say how likely they were to work with non-indigenous minority languages in the future. The results are highly encouraging, as Table 5 shows.

| Likelihood | Number |
|------------|--------|
| very likely | 41 |
| possibly | 10 |
| unsure | 5 |
| probably not | 9 |
| very unlikely | 1 |

**Table 5.** Likelihood of respondents working on non-indigenous minority languages in the future

In addition to wishing to work on such languages, there was a good fit between the languages the linguists and language engineers wanted to work on and those being worked on by the translators, as shown in Table 6.

| Language | Number of linguists/ language engineers wishing to work on this language | Translators working on this language |
|----------|-----------------------------------------------------------|--------------------------------------|
| Chinese | 28 | 4 |
| Arabic | 19 | 2 |
| Hindi | 18 | 3 |
| Vietnamese | 17 | 0 |
| Tamil | 15 | 1 |
| Farsi | 11 | 0 |
| Urdu | 11 | 5 |
| Gujarati | 10 | 0 |
| Bengali | 9 | 2 |
| Panjabi | 9 | 2 |
| Singhalese | 6 | 0 |
| Sylheti | 4 | 0 |
| Somali | 3 | 0 |

**Table 6.** Fit between language interests of translators and linguists

Language engineers wanted corpus data to work on seven of the 14 languages which the translators surveyed work upon. More importantly, if we exclude European languages on which the translators are working (for which some corpus data exists) the language engineers want to work on seven of the ten non-indigenous minority languages translated in the UK translation agencies we surveyed. With findings such as these we can help to inform the process of corpus creation geared towards translation studies and practices, to ensure that the corpora being constructed represent both the full range of languages currently being translated in Europe and to meet the research needs of language engineers and linguists wishing to work on those languages.

## 5.    Conclusion

What the questionnaires show is that the level of interest from the language engineering community in working with minority languages is high: in the past 10 years or so corpus linguistics has tended to be based mainly around West European languages such as English, French, German and Spanish. It is now clear that the landscape is changing - the response rate to the questionnaire was high, and the range of languages specified was large – with South Asian languages, traditionally ignored by corpus linguistics, finally starting to attract attention. This is a crucial expansion of the focus of corpus linguistics, as these are languages which are important for domestic translation tasks in the UK. If the survey was broadened beyond the UK it is undoubtedly the case that slightly different sets of languages would figure as being important to domestic translators. But the essential message would remain fairly constant – indigenous European languages are relatively well served with corpus data in comparison to non-indigenous European languages, yet non-indigenous European languages are important foci for domestic translation activities in Europe. This is not to say that all work on indigenous European languages should be abandoned. As noted at the beginning of this paper, there is much room for improvement in the provision of such corpus data at present. However, the provision of corpus data for the study of non-indigenous minority languages is generally poorer, and hence is deserving of attention.

Arising from our survey work we have begun the process of providing corpora to enable the study of non-indigenous minority languages in the UK. The EPSRC has funded a project entitled Enabling Minority

Language Engineering[6] which has the explicit goal of providing basic monolingual spoken and written corpus data for UK non-indigenous minority languages as well as suitable parallel corpus data. It is hoped that in the near future, as a consequence of this work, non-indigenous languages in the UK will at least be on an equal footing with indigenous languages. If this paper can present a hope for the future, it is that similar actions in countries across Europe can help to expand the range of languages for which resources are available, widening the set of resources available to those engaged in domestic translation tasks irrespective of whether the language concerned is indigenous to Europe or not.

# References

Erjavec, Tomaž, Nancy Ide, Vladimir Petkevic and Jean Véronis (1995) 'Multext-East: Multilingual Text Tools and Corpora for Central and Eastern European Languages', *TELRI, Proceedings of the First European Seminar, 'Language Resources for Language Technologies'*, Tihany (Hungary), September 1995, 87-97.

Kordoni, Valia (2000) *Stylebook for the English Treebank in Verbmobil*, Technical report, Eberhard-Karls-Universitat Tubingen, Tubingen.

McEnery, Tony and Andrew Wilson (1994) 'Corpora and Translation: Uses and Future Prospects', in Michèle Lorgnet (ed) *Atti della Fiera Internazionale della Traduzione II*, Bologna: CLUEB, 246-355.

------, Andrew Wilson, Fernando Sanchez Leon, and Amalio F. Nieto Serrano (1997) 'Multilingual Resources for European Languages: Contributions of the Crater Project', *Literary and Linguistic Computing* 12(4): 219-226.

------, Paul Baker and Lou Burnard (2000) 'Corpus Resources and Minority Language Engineering', in Maria Gavrilidou, George Carayannis, Stella Markantontou, Stelios Piperidis and Gregory Stainhauoer (eds) *Proceedings of the Second International Conference on Language Resources and Evaluation*, Athens, Greece, 801-806.

Stegmann, Rosemary, Heike Schulz and Erhard W. Hinrichs (1998) *Stylebook for the German Treebank in VERBMOBIL*. Technical Report, Universitat Tubingen.

Véronis, Jean and Liliane Khouri (1995) 'Etiquetage Grammatical Multilingue: le Projet Multext', *Traitement Automatique des Langues* 36(1/2): 233-248.

---

[6] Funded by the UK EPSRC, project reference GR/N19106.

# Appendix 1

## Translators Questionnaire

Please answer the questions below as fully as you can. Your answers will help us in our study of the process of translation in the non-indigenous minority languages of the U.K. The questionnaire is completely anonymous and the answers will only be used for the purposes of academic research.

1. What community languages do you translate? (Please list all of them.)
2. How long have you been doing this kind of work?
3. Have you had training for the work you do? Please describe it briefly (e.g. Diploma in Community Interpreting and Translation, DPSI etc).
4. Approximately how many pieces of written translation work have you done? (If you translate more than one language, please note them down separately).
   - In the last year?
   - In the last three months
5. Please mention some examples of the main kinds of translation you have done (e.g. health leaflets, marriage certificates, policy statements)
6. Do you have access in your work to any of the following?
   ☐ a bilingual dictionary (in book form)?
   ☐ a monolingual English dictionary (in book form)?
   ☐ a monolingual dictionary in another language (in book form – please name the language)
   ☐ an English language word processor (please give the name of the software)
   ☐ a word processor in another language (please name the language and the software)
   ☐ an English language spell-checker (please give the name of the software)
   ☐ a spell-checker in another language (please give the name of the language and the software)
   ☐ an English language online dictionary (please give the name of the software)
   ☐ an online dictionary in another language (please name the language and the software)

☐   other English language translator's tools (please state which)

☐   translator's tools for other languages (please give details i.e. thesaurus, science/legal terminology database, computer-assisted translation program)

7.   Do you find information technology (e.g. word processing software, online dictionaries) useful to you in your work as a translator? Please explain why or why not.

8.   Are there types of computer software that you've used for translation in the past but don't use anymore? Please list them and explain why you no longer use them.

9.   If you've used several types of computer software in the past, which one do you prefer and why?

10.  Are you satisfied with the information technology which is available to you as a translator for:
     a) English (please give details of why or why not)
     b) The other languages you translate? (Please give details of why or why not)

11.  Please tell us about the process of producing the translation by ticking ANY of the following statements which are generally true.

☐   I normally write out the translation by hand

☐   I normally type out the translation on a typewriter

☐   I normally give the translation to someone else to word process

☐   I normally word process the translation myself

☐   The final version of the translation is normally typed out

☐   The final version of my translation is normally hand-written

☐   I normally save the final processed version of my translation on disc or computer

12.  Is there anything else about translation that you would like to mention that we might have missed? Please use the space below. If not, thanks for completing the survey.

*Tony McEnery, Mark Sebba, Paul Baker, Mabel Lie. Department of Linguistics, Lancaster University.*

# Student Translation Archive
## Design, Development and Application

LYNNE BOWKER AND PETER BENNISON

*This paper describes the creation of the Student Translation Archive (STA) and Student Translation Tracking System (STTS) currently being used to collect, manage and study texts that have been translated by students. In addition, it outlines a preliminary methodology for exploiting the STA by extracting different types of corpora that may be useful or interesting in a translator training context. Some of the difficulties encountered during the development of the prototype system are outlined, as well as plans for future development.*

## 1. Introduction

For a number of years, foreign language teachers have been compiling and studying learner corpora, which are defined as textual databases of the language produced by foreign language learners (e.g. Granger 1993, 1998). Such corpora are used to identify typical characteristics of texts produced by language learners and to identify errors and problem areas that can then be addressed as part of the language learning curriculum.

Student translators can be considered as a highly specialized type of language learner/user. Although their specific needs differ from those of foreign language learners, a similar approach to collecting and studying the output of student translators would be highly valuable for both pedagogical and research applications. With regard to pedagogy, a corpus of student translations can provide a means of identifying areas of difficulty that could then be integrated into the curriculum and discussed in class. In terms of research, scholars such as Baker (1995, 1996) and Laviosa (1998) have already demonstrated that corpora can be useful for studying the nature of professionally translated texts; we believe that there is also much to be learned about translation process and product by investigating the nature of texts translated by students.

The aim of this paper is to describe the design, development and application of the Student Translation Archive (STA) and Student Translation Tracking System (STTS). One of the authors, Lynne Bowker, has been involved in the teaching of specialized translation for a number of years, and during this time, she has been laying the foundations for the design, compilation and exploitation of STA and STTS. The second author, Peter Bennison, is a software developer who has implemented working prototypes of STA and STTS. This paper is divided into five main sections. Section 1 provides some background information about the beginnings of the project, the initial ad hoc collection of student translations, and some of the difficulties encountered during early stages of work on the STA. Section 2 outlines the more formalized design of the STA. Section 3 discusses the development of the prototype STTS, describing some of the problems encountered. Section 4 presents a number of applications of STA and STTS. Finally, section 5 outlines some plans for future development.

## 2.  Background

Translator trainers are constantly collecting translations from students, correcting them and handing them back. In addition to evaluating each text in its own right, trainers frequently attempt to compare multiple texts. For example, trainers may try to compare different translations of the same text done by different students in the same class in order to try to identify common areas of difficulty, or they may attempt to compare several pieces of work done by the same student in order to gauge that student's progress over the semester. However, such comparisons are difficult to make when working with paper documents. For instance, an average-sized desk is simply not large enough to spread out thirty different translations so trainers are constantly shuffling paper and losing track of where they are. Furthermore, since trainers typically return the corrected texts to the students, they must rely on memory or on cryptic notes for conducting any type of longitudinal study of a student's progress.

These types of frustrating experiences led us to believe that there simply must be a better way to gather and manage student translation data. The work being carried out with learner corpora in the field of foreign language learning (e.g. Altenberg 1997; Granger 1993, 1998) inspired us to compile an electronic collection of student translations, which we now refer to as the Student Translation Archive (STA). The accompanying management software, known as the Student Translation Tracking System (STTS), allows users to extract corpora from the STA according to specific criteria. The distinction between an archive and a corpus is neatly summarized by Barnbrook (1996:23), who explains that "The collection of computer-readable language that you assemble for your project, selected on the basis of your research criteria, is usually referred to as a corpus, to distinguish it from the more random collections of texts held in text archives."

Initial work on this project began in 1997 when students were asked to voluntarily submit electronic copies of their translations (e.g. on diskette or via e-mail) in addition to handing in hard copies. Students were not obliged to submit their work for inclusion in the STA; however, in our experience, many of them were willing to do so. They were also asked to provide some additional attribute information that would make it possible to extract corpora from the STA by selecting texts that match a set of predefined attributes. These attributes are listed in Table 1.

| Attribute | Description |
|---|---|
| Source Text Reference | Allows a target text to be related back to a particular source text |
| Student ID Number | Allows user to identify all the work done by a particular student |
| Course Code | Allows user to identify all the work done for a particular course NOTE: a course code, such as TRA4530, provides the following information: a) the source and target language of the translation (e.g. English to French), b) the level of the course (e.g. 4th year), and c) the broad subject field of the course (e.g. legal translation) |
| Date | Allows user to extract work done during a particular time frame |
| Translation Conditions | Allows user to distinguish between translations done simply as homework, those done for a graded assessment (i.e., where students may have made a more concerted effort), or those done under exam-like conditions (i.e., within strict time constraints or with limited access to resources) |
| Native Language | Allows user to identify a student's native language (e.g. to determine if there has been interference from this language, to determine if students are translating into or out of their native language) |
| Dominant Foreign Language | Allows user to identify a student's dominant foreign language |
| Other Foreign Language(s) | Allows user to identify other foreign languages used by a student |

**Table 1**. Attributes accompanying each translation in the STA

## 2.1 Difficulties encountered

One of the first difficulties encountered during the initial data collection effort was that students used a variety of different software packages to prepare their translations. Therefore, translations were received in a variety of formats (e.g. MS-Word, WordPerfect, Macintosh, etc.) – some of which could not easily be handled.

A second difficulty was that students recorded the attribute information in a variety of ways. For instance, when recording information for the attribute 'Native Language', English-speaking students used a variety of notations, including 'English', 'Eng.', 'En', 'EN', and 'E'. The lack of consistency in recording this data meant that it would be difficult to automate searches. In addition, sometimes students would neglect to fill in the data for all the attribute fields.

Finally, the fact that information was submitted via e-mail attachment (or occasionally on diskette) meant that the translator trainer spent a lot of time doing menial tasks, such as opening messages, converting file formats, standardizing the notation of attribute information, chasing down missing information, copying, pasting and saving the data into a new file.

## 3. STA design

Faced with the difficulties described above, the decision was made to formalize and automate the collection process as much as possible. At this time, Peter Bennison, a software developer with experience building databases, joined the project.

## 3.1 Entry template

The first step was to design and construct an entry template. This was done to ensure that students used the same file format and that information was entered in a consistent manner. It was decided to use MS-Word to build the template: MS-Word was the most commonly used word processor among the students, it was available in the computer labs on campus, and it was possible to program an MS-Word template using Visual Basic for Applications (VBA), which is a programming language that is part of the MS-Office suite. Furthermore, an MS-Word template could be easily integrated with the MS-Access database package that was used to build the prototype STA.

The template contains a number of features. Firstly, it provides drop down lists for most of the attributes, which means that instead of entering information in free-format (e.g. 'English' or 'Eng' or 'EN' or 'E') students need only select the appropriate information from a list of pre-defined attributes. Only two fields do not come with pre-defined attributes: the 'student ID' field and the 'Translation' field (i.e., the field where the student enters the target text). Secondly, the template provides a validation feature, which means that students are prompted to fill in each of the fields before closing the file. If a student attempts to close a file without filling in an attribute field, a message box will pop up advising the student which field(s) still need to be filled in, as shown in (Figure 1). Thirdly, the template saves all the files in plain text format (.txt), which means they can be easily processed by other software (e.g. corpus analysis tools) at a later stage.

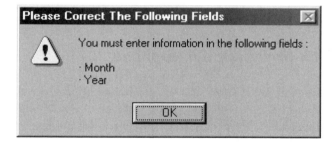

**Figure 1.** A validation feature prompts students to fill in
all the attribute fields before closing a file

## 3.2 Difficulties encountered during the development of the entry template

The entry template is edited separately from the database. If new information needs to be added to the template (e.g. a new source text reference, a new course code), then the template must be edited directly and a copy of the updated version must be supplied to the students.

It should also be noted that the template uses macros, which may be viewed by some as a security flaw. New versions of MS-Office (i.e., Office 2000 and above) have a default setting that disables all macros within templates. This is a somewhat draconian yet effective security measure against computer viruses written in VBA. In order to permit macros to run and thereby be able to use the template, users will need to adjust their security settings. Therefore, students who wish to use the template in order to contribute to the STA will need to be told how to adjust their settings and they should be advised to have current anti-virus software to protect their files.

## 3.3 Batch import program

In order to get the individual translations into the STA, a program was written in the Perl programming language to automate the batch import process. All the files (i.e., the translations) must be stored in a logical directory structure, and then the batch import program goes through the directory, opens each file, reads the indexing information (i.e., the attributes), and creates comma separated value (CSV) files, which can then be imported directly into MS-Access tables. This means that indexing information does not need to be retyped whenever a new translation is added to the STA.

# 4.  STTS prototype development

The next stage in this project was the development of a tool that would allow a user to interact with the STA by adding or modifying information or by extracting corpora; this tool is known as the Student Translation Tracking System (STTS). STTS allows users to modify or add to the contents of the STA (e.g. source texts and corresponding student translations) using a simple graphical user interface as shown in (Figure 2).

STTS also contains a query form, shown in Figure 3, which allows users to extract corpora from the STA. Users can specify any combination of attributes (see Table 1) and STTS will retrieve all the texts that match the specified criteria. Users can then choose to export some or all of these texts to a separate file, and the resulting corpus can then be investigated using corpus analysis software such as *Wordsmith Tools* (Scott 1996) or *MonoConc* (Barlow 1999).

## 4.1  Difficulties encountered during STTS development

STTS was originally developed using VBA and MS-Access because we felt this would be an easy-to-use database program and hoped to be able to recommend this approach to non-technical people interested in setting

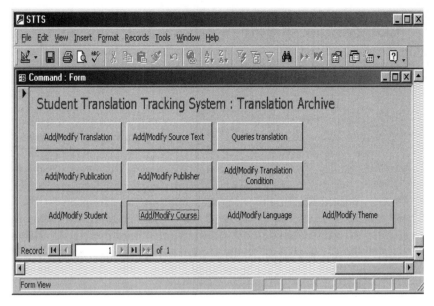

**Figure 2.** The user interface of STTS allows users to add to
or modify the contents of the STA

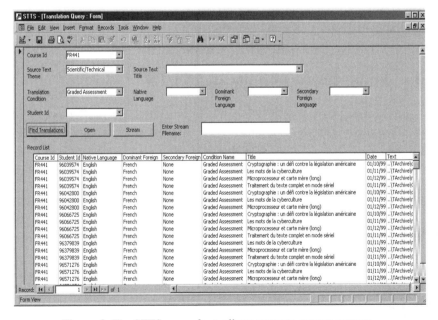

**Figure 3.** The STTS query form allows users to extract corpora
from the STA according to any combination of attributes

up similar applications (e.g. translator trainers who have minimal programming experience or limited technical support at their institution).
Although MS-Access has some useful features (e.g. table design wizards,
user-interface design wizards), when working with this package, we discovered that it also has a number of drawbacks, including:

- limitations (e.g. it is not possible to dynamically resize a list in a
  user interface form; it is not possible to add a hyperlink field to a
  record within a list)
- idiosyncrasies (e.g. the programmer must manually add line continu-
  ation characters (& _); user-defined procedures and event procedures
  are called differently than in other programming languages)
- bugs (e.g. many queries created in the query editor did not work in
  the VBA code; queries that did work sometimes produced variable
  results (i.e., the record set returned by a query in one instance would
  be different than the set returned for the same query in another
  instance).

On a positive note, the integration between user interface controls and
VBA code worked reasonably well. The ability of a list to automatically
run a query on the database and display the results was effective; however, the difficulties encountered while trying to get it to work effectively
and consistently detracted from this attractive feature.

## 5.   Applications of STA and STTS

In this section, we will outline a number of different types of corpora that
can be extracted from the STA with the help of STTS. This list is by no
means exhaustive; it simply contains suggestions for types of corpora that
have, in our experience, proved to be useful or interesting in a translator
training context. A number of these applications are aimed at helping translator trainers to direct their own teaching practices, whereas others might
also be of interest to students, who may, for example, wish to monitor
their own progress.

### 5.1  Text-specific corpora

A trainer can extract a corpus consisting of all the translations of a given
source text done by the students in a particular class. Using a corpus analysis tool (e.g. *Wordsmith Tools*, *MonoConc*), the trainer can then go on to

examine corresponding sections of all the translations simultaneously. This allows the trainer to identify areas where the class as a whole is having difficulty, as distinct from problems that may have befallen only one or two students. Identifying such patterns is much more difficult and cumbersome when working with separate sheets of paper.

For example, as shown in Table 2, using the corpus analysis programme *Wordsmith Tools*, we were able to isolate various translations of the following source text segment that was taken from an article entitled "Le DVD tient ses promesses" which was published in a semi-specialized periodical called *Sciences et avenir* (February 1998):

> Premier enfant d'un accord entre géants de la micro-informatique et de la vidéo, le DVD, un nouveau standard, propose une capacité de stockage exceptionnelle, équivalent à 3000 disquettes de 1,4 Mo ou à plus de sept CD-Rom!

| |
|---|
| The product of a joint initiative between computer and video industry powers, the DVD sets new standards with an exceptional memory capacity equivalent to 3,000 1.4MB floppy disks or more than seven CD-ROMs. |
| The first result of projects between micro computing and video giants, DVD, a new standard, has an excellent memory capacity, equivalent to 3,000 1.4 MB diskettes or more than 7 CD-ROMs! |
| The brainchild of an agreement between the big names in micro-processors and in video, the DVD, a new standard, offers an exceptional storage capacity, equivalent to 3000 diskettes of 1,4 MB or more than seven CD-ROMs! |
| DVD is the first offering of a combination of the giants of micro-computing and video. DVD is a new standard and offers a huge storage capacity equivalent to 3000 X 1.4 meg floppies or more than seven CD-ROMs! |
| The brainchild of an agreement between the micro-computing and video giants, the DVD, a new standard in technology, offers an extraordinary storage capacity - equivalent to 3000 1.4 Mb disks or more than 7 CD-ROM. |
| The new-born from an emergence between micro-computing and video giants, DVD, or Digital Versatile Disc is the new standard offering exceptional storage capacity equivalent to 3000 diskettes of 1.4 MB or more than 7 CD ROM. |
| The first child of a positive agreement between giants of the micro-computing and video industry, the DVD is a new development which has an exceptional memory capacity equivalent to 3,000 diskettes of 1.4Mb or more than 7 CD-ROM! |
| The brainchild of an agreement between microcomputing and video giants, the DVD, a new phenomenon, proposes an exceptional storage capacity equivalent to that of 3,000 diskettes of 1.4 MB or at most seven CD-ROM! |
| The brain child born of a deal between the micro-computing and video giants, the DVD sets a new standard by offering an exceptional storage capacity, equivalent to 3000 diskettes of 1.4 Mb or more than 7 CD-ROM! |
| The first child of a promising union between giants of the micro-computing and video industries, the DVD is a new innovation offering exceptional memory capacity, equivalent to 3,000 1.4mb floppy discs or more than seven CD-ROMs. |

**Table 2.** A selection of different student translations of the same source text segment

By examining these different translations simultaneously, we were able to determine, for instance, that the class as a whole would benefit from 1) a discussion regarding the pluralization of abbreviations (since many students did not pluralize the abbreviation 'CD-ROM'); and 2) a discussion on the distinction between the concepts 'storage' and 'memory' (since a number of students mistakenly translated *capacité de stockage* as 'memory capacity' instead of 'storage capacity'). In contrast, we could see that other problems were specific to only one or two students, such as 1) the failure of one student to change the comma to a period in the decimal number '1.4'; and 2) the decision of one student to use the spoken language abbreviation 'meg' for the term 'megabyte' instead of the standard written abbreviation 'MB'.

## 5.2 Subject-field specific corpora

Many translation courses are devoted to specialized subject fields, such as medical translation or legal translation. Trainers can extract a corpus of translations pertaining to a particular subject field and examine these to determine if a problem is specific to one particular source text or if it is a difficulty that is also manifesting itself in other texts dealing with a related subject.

For example, over the course of a semester, students in a technical translation class had to translate a number of different texts explaining how optical scanners work. The first text was from a semi-specialized computer magazine and it explained the concepts in an accessible manner that the majority of students clearly understood and were able to render adequately. Another text, which the students translated several weeks after the first, contained the same basic information, but it was expressed in a more abstract and convoluted way. This time, many of the students seemed less sure of themselves, did not appear to understand the concepts in question, and stuck much more closely to the syntax of the original. As a result, the translations were less accurate and less readable. The fact that the first translation had been fairly accurately rendered seems to indicate that the students were generally able to comprehend the subject matter; therefore, the difficulties with the later text were more likely to be caused by the language and style that were used. The trainer therefore decided to spend more class time discussing stylistic features of different text types rather than explaining the subject matter itself (i.e., how optical scanners work).

## 5.3  Corpora spanning multiple subject fields

Corpora that span multiple subject fields can be extracted from the STA
to investigate whether the problems encountered by a group of students in
one type of specialized translation course (e.g. technical translation) are
similar to or different from the problems they are having in another type
of specialized translation course (e.g. economic translation). In this way,
a trainer can try to determine whether a student is having a problem that
manifests itself regardless of the subject field and therefore needs to be
tackled at a more global level, or whether the student is having difficulty
caused by a lack of knowledge of some aspect of a particular subject field
(e.g. concepts, vocabulary, syntax) and which does not manifest itself
when working in other fields.

For example, in examining translations produced by a student taking
both an economic translation course and a technical translation course, it
became clear that the student had a general difficulty in grasping the concepts of register and text type. In the economic translation class, the student
had translated a section from an annual report produced by an investment
company, while in the technical translation class, the student had translated an extract from a technical report describing a new computer
operating system. Both translations contained inappropriate constructions
(e.g. use of contractions, use of the second person, sentence fragments).
The trainer therefore decided to approach the problem independently of
any particular subject field.

## 5.4  Cross-linguistic/same subject field corpora

Corpora that cover the same subject field in different languages can also
be extracted in order to examine the impact of source language (SL) interference. For example, a student may be following two different courses in
technical translation: one from Spanish into English and one from French
into English. A comparison of the two sets of translations may reveal that
the student is having different types of problems when translating out of
Spanish than when translating out of French, in which case it may be
necessary to focus on SL interference, or it may turn out that the student
is having similar problems regardless of the SL (e.g. perhaps the student
has not grasped the concept of register), in which case it may be necessary to tackle the issue in a non-SL related way.

For example, a student translated two texts on the subject of Digital Versatile Disks (DVDs) in the same semester: one from Spanish into English and one from French into English. As illustrated in Table 3, in both cases some of the student's terminological choices have been influenced by the source text in question. For instance, the Spanish term *puntos* has been translated by 'points', while the French term *trous* has been translated by 'holes'; however, in both cases, a better translation would have been 'pits'. Similarly, the Spanish term *micras* has been left as 'micras' in the English translation, while the symbol 'µm' in the French text has been incorrectly rendered as 'um'; in both cases, either 'microns' or 'micrometers' would have been a better solution.

| Source text in Spanish (extract from "¿Cómo Funciona un DVD?", Jumping, julio-agosto 1999) | En primer lugar se ha reducido y compactado el tramado de puntos que se asientan sobre la superficie del disco. Para conseguir incluir más información en prácticamente el mismo espacio, ha sido necesario reducir sustancialmente el tamaño de los puntos (de 0.83 a 0.4 micras), asi como la distancia existente entre éstos (de 1.6 a 0.74 micras), lo que da lugar a una mayor densidad de grabación. |
|---|---|
| Student's translation into English (December 1999) | Firstly, the layout of points on the surface of the disk has been reduced and compacted. In order to store more information in practically the same space, it has been necessary to substantially reduce the size of the points (0.83 to 0.4 micras) as well as the distance between the points (1.6 to 0.74 micras) which provides a greater recording density. |
| Source text in French (extract from "Le DVD tient ses promesses", Sciences et Avenir, février 1999) | La différence entre DVD et CD réside dans la taille des trous: 0,83 µm pour le CD, 0,40 µm pour le DVD, et la distance entre les pistes (respectivement 1,60 µ:m et 0,74 µm). Cette réduction multiplie par trois la densité de données enregistrables par couche. |
| Student's translation into English (December 1999) | The difference between DVD and CD is the size of the holes, 0.83um in the CD and 0.4 in the DVD, and the distance between the tracks, 1.6um and 0.74 respectively. This reduction means three times more recording density per layer. |

**Table 3.** Examples of two translations done by the same student that show evidence of SL interference

## 5.5  Longitudinal corpora

Longitudinal studies can be carried out to chart the progress of individual students or groups of students, and they can be done over the course of a semester, a year or even an entire degree. Using such a corpus, a trainer (or even a student) can see which problems appear to have been resolved and which are still causing difficulties.

For example, at the beginning of the academic year, a second year student was identified as having a tendency to overuse the definite article (i.e., 'the') when translating from French into English. However, as summarized in Table 4, over the course of the year the student's translations showed a decrease in the use of the definite article after receiving feedback and reinforcement from the trainer.

| | Source texts (French) | | Target texts (English) | |
|---|---|---|---|---|
| | Total number of words in ST | Number of definite articles (le/la/l'/les) | Total number of words in TT | Number of definite articles ('the') |
| Text 1 (Sept 1998) | 236 | 22 | 223 | 31 |
| Text 2 (Dec1998) | 252 | 21 | 235 | 20 |
| Text 3 (April 1999) | 272 | 28 | 247 | 13 |

**Table 4.** A longitudinal study of a student's use of the definite article when translating from French into English

Another type of longitudinal study could be conducted if a trainer decides to try a new teaching method from one year to the next. If the trainer has used the same source text (or even different texts that pose similar translation difficulties) with more than one group of students, it may be interesting for the trainer to compare the translations done by a class who were taught using the 'old' method with those of a class who were taught using the 'new' method. While a comparison of this sort would not be enough to allow the trainer to make definitive claims about the usefulness of one teaching method over another, it may nevertheless reveal some interesting points worthy of further investigation.

## 6. Future developments

The experiments conducted with the STA and STTS prototypes were very positive, but they were also a learning experience. Based on this experience, we have begun to make some modifications and improvements.

As outlined in section 3.1, we encountered some difficulties with the VBA programming language. To help overcome these problems, we are in the process of re-implementing the code in the Java programming language. Java is a more robust language than VBA, and it is also non-platform specific, which means that the system will be able to run under different operating systems.

Another notable weakness with the current prototype set-up is the fact that it operates in stand-alone mode. This means that the STA is accessible only on a single computer and all the translations are sent to one trainer who is responsible for inputting them – a job that can be time consuming and labour intensive. In order to improve the system, we are in the process of developing it as a Web-based application using a client-server model. This means that it will be possible to access the STA from any computer that has an Internet connection. Instead of e-mailing texts to a single trainer who must input them all, students can enter their own texts directly into the STA via a browser client and they will be stored on a Web server. This means that the trainer no longer needs to act as the 'middle person' for entering data. Part of the client server model will require user authentication both for entering new translations and for querying the STA. Users will be organized into different groups (e.g. trainers, students, system administrator) and these groups can be assigned different types of user privileges (e.g. read-only, read/write, etc.). A further advantage of the Web-based application is that the system administrator will be able to edit the Web form that is used to submit new translations to the STA so this page will always be up-to-date.

Quality control is another important issue. In the prototype system, a trainer is responsible for entering the texts into the STA and so this trainer can verify that the content is acceptable (i.e., that the students are not submitting inappropriate material); however, with the new Web-based application, students can enter their own texts directly. In order to protect the integrity of the STA, texts entered by students will first be directed to a sort of 'holding tank' and these will be screened by the system administrator before being sent to the STA.

Other modifications currently under consideration include having an XML interface in order to allow other data analysis programs to interact with the STA, and the encoding of different types of student errors within the translated texts in order to facilitate data analysis.

# Acknowledgements

We would like to thank the students at both Dublin City University and the University of Ottawa who have contributed their work to the STA, as well as those who participated in the translation experiments. Development of the STA and STTS was funded in part by an Albert College Research Fellowship awarded by Dublin City University and by a research grant from the University of Ottawa Academic Development Fund.

# References

Altenberg, Bengt (1997) 'Exploring the Swedish Component of the International Corpus of Learner English', in Barbara Lewandowska-Tomaszczyk and Patrick J. Melia (eds) *Proceedings of PALC '97: Practical Applications in Language Corpora*, Łódź: Łódź University Press, 119-132.

Baker, Mona (1995) 'Corpora in Translation Studies: An Overview and Some Suggestions for Future Research', *Target* 7(2): 223-243.

------ (1996) 'Corpus-based Translation Studies: The Challenges that Lie Ahead', in Harold L. Somers (ed) *Terminology, LSP and Translation: Studies in Language Engineering in Honour of Juan C. Sager*, Amsterdam and Philadelphia: John Benjamins, 175-186.

Barlow, Michael (1999) *MonoConc*, Houston, TX: Athelstan.

Barnbrook, Geoff (1996) *Language and Computers*, Edinburgh: Edinburgh University Press.

Granger, Sylviane (1993) 'The International Corpus of Learner English', in Jan Aarts, Pieter de Haan and Nelleke Oostdijk (eds) *English Language Corpora: Design, Analysis and Exploitation*, Rodopi: Amsterdam, 57-69.

------ (1998) (ed) *Learner English on Computer*, London: Longman.

Laviosa, Sara (1998) 'The English Comparable Corpus: A Resource and a Methodology', in Lynne Bowker, Michael Cronin, Dorothy Kenny and Jennifer Pearson (eds) *Unity in Diversity? Current Trends in Translation Studies*, Manchester: St. Jerome, 101-112.

Scott, Mike (1996) *Wordsmith Tools*, Oxford: Oxford University Press.

# On a Pseudo-subversive Use of Corpora in Translator Training

KIRSTEN MALMKJÆR

*The use in translation studies of methodologies inspired by corpus linguistics has proved to be one of the most important gate-openers to progress in the discipline since Toury's re-thinking of the concept of equivalence. In this paper, I discuss mainly the use of corpora in translator education, arguing that, the many advantages to be had by this method notwithstanding, there are problems. For example, it is not always obvious which corpus might help a translator solve a specific problem; corpus evidence might be misleading in some cases; and offering past linguistic behaviour as a model for the future flies in the face of the nature of language and may, furthermore, stifle invention. For these reasons, I argue, it is worth exploring ways of using corpora which may seem subversive of standard uses, either alone or in conjunction with more traditional methods of investigation and teaching in Translation Studies.*

## 1. Introduction

The use in translation studies of methodologies inspired by corpus linguistics has proved to be one of the most important gate-openers to progress in the discipline since Toury's (1980) re-thinking of the concept of equivalence; advances made through their use in descriptive, theoretical and pedagogical approaches to translation are well known and well documented (see e.g. Baker 1995; Laviosa 1998; Zanettin 1998, *Meta* 1998).

In this paper, I shall be mainly concerned with the use of corpora in translator education, and I shall argue that as well as the standard and extremely valuable ways of using corpora in translator training described in sources such as those referred to above and elsewhere in this volume, it is worth exploring ways of using corpora which may seem subversive of standard uses, either alone or in conjunction with more traditional methods of investigation and teaching in Translation Studies. I think it is important to do this for two reasons. One is that there are real-life translation problems which corpora cannot help us with if we stick to the standard methods and the standard corpora; the other is that we must make sure that we demonstrate to students that standard uses of corpora in translation studies are based on an assumption which is blatantly false, and which we know to be false, but which we nevertheless pretend to make for good reason. We need to be open on this issue lest students discover the pretence for themselves without discovering its justification, and are tempted to dismiss corpora altogether.

## 2.  Some common assumptions connected with corpus construction and exploitation

Among the commonly held assumptions underlying corpus construction and the use of corpora in translator training (and also in language teaching and translating) are:

- that language is patterned (see e.g. Baker 1996: 176)
- that language users are *very* bad at introspecting what the (lexical/ collocational) patterns are in actual language use (see e.g. Sinclair and Renouf 1988: 151-2; Sinclair 1991: 39)
- that the patterns are laid bare in corpora of language in use (Baker 1996: 176; Sinclair and Renouf 1988: 151-2; Sinclair 1991: 39)
- that the future will (and should) be like the past.

The last assumption is implicit in many (though not all) suggestions for applications of corpus linguistics to teaching. For example, Baker (1995: 231) declares that:

> Their [corpora of SL-TL pairs] most important contribution to the discipline in general is that they support a shift of emphasis, from *prescription* to *description*. They allow us to establish, objectively, how translators overcome difficulties of translation in practice and to use this evidence to provide realistic models for trainee translators.

Clearly the idea that past translators' choices should provide a model for trainees assumes that future use should be modelled on past practice, and it is, we might note in passing, just about as prescriptive as it is possible to be. The same difficulty besets claims that descriptive grammars are not prescriptive: they may not be meant prescriptively, but put them in the hands of a teacher or a learner, and prescription – if not explicit then certainly implicit – is very likely to follow. But while the distinction between description and prescription is probably almost always spurious where pedagogy is concerned, a distinction between claims made on the basis of empirically derived data and claims made on the basis of introspection is certainly not; it is in this respect that corpora excel and offer a solution to the pedagogical conundrum created by the combination of the two assumptions at the top of the list above: that language is patterned (assumption 1) but that people, including teachers and materials writers, are not good at introspecting what the patterns actually are (assumption 2).

The evidence available to support these two assumptions is overwhelming, so anything that helps us live tranquil lives in spite of them is a most welcome addition to our pedagogical resource-box. However, just as no pedagogical method will suit all students equally well, no pedagogical aid can be used to solve all problems, and corpora present two related difficulties: (1) It is not always clear exactly which type of corpus might be able to help a translator with a specific translation problem; (2) unless used inventively sometimes, corpora cannot help us to act creatively; yet much translational activity requires creativity. Both these problems arise from the same, more basic difficulty which is shared by any method which relies on applications of captive linguistic data, namely, that the fourth assumption on our list – that the linguistic future will and should resemble the past – simply cannot be sustained. Beyond the extremely minimalist stability now thought to define human language (Chomsky 1995), it has no basis in either the facts of linguistic behaviour or in semantic theory. It is a fiction required to sustain descriptive linguistics and language pedagogy, and while it should be vigorously supported as such, all tendencies to assign it factual status ought to be equally strongly resisted.

To see the first problem in action (that it is not always clear which corpus might be used to help a translator faced with a specific translation problem), consider the problem of selecting translation equivalents for the two adjectives I have left untranslated in their occurrences in the story I present in the following section.

## 3.   Case study 1

The following is my translation of Hans Christian Andersen's story "Prindsesses paa Ærten" (written in 1835). I have left untranslated the occurrences in it of two adjectives which seem to me to raise questions that a translator of this story may need help to solve (see also Knowles and Malmkjær 1991; Malmkjær 1993; Malmkjær 1995):

## The princess on the pea

There was once a prince; he wanted to have a princess, but she would have to be a *rigtig* princess. So he travelled all around the world to find one, but everywhere something was wrong, there were plenty of princesses, but whether they were *rigtige* princesses he could not quite figure out, there was always something which was not so *rigtigt*. So then he came home again and was very sad, for he wanted so much to have a *virkelig* princess.

Then one evening there was a dreadful storm; there was thunder and lightening, the rain poured down, it was quite frightful! Then someone knocked on the town gate, and the old king went to open it.

It was a princess who was standing outside. But God what a sight she was with the rain and the evil weather! Water was running down her hair and her clothes, and it was running in at the toes of her shoes and out at the heels, and yet she said that she was a *virkelig* princess.

"Well, we'll soon see about that!" thought the old queen, but she didn't say anything, went into the bedroom, took all the bedclothes off and laid a pea on the bottom of the bed, then she took twenty mattresses, laid them on top of the pea, and then another twenty eiderdown quilts on top of the mattresses.

That was where the princess was to lie that night.

In the morning they asked her how she had slept.

"Oh, frightfully badly!" said the princess, "I have hardly closed my eyes the whole night! God knows what there was in the bed? I have been lying on something hard, so that I am quite black and blue all over my body! It is quite frightful!"

Then they could see that she was a *rigtig* princess as she had been able to feel the pea through the twenty mattresses and the twenty eiderdown quilts. No-one but a *virkelig* princess could be that tender skinned.

So the prince took her as his wife, for now he knew that he had a *rigtig* princess, and the pea was put in the Royal Collection, where it is still to be seen, if no-one has taken it.

You see that was a *rigtig* story!

There is one instance of the adjective *rigtig* which I will not discuss further here: the third instance. Its most obvious translation into English in its context is 'right'; but in standard English, this word cannot be used for the other uses of the adjective *rigtig* in this story: whereas 'a right princess' is fine in some Scottish varieties of English, in the standard dialect it is deviant, and my translation is into the standard. Therefore, the affinity between this instance and the rest in the Source Text has to be foregone in the Target Text (at least, I have decided not to try to retain it).

There are two obvious questions which would occur to most translators of this story: the two adjectives *rigtig* and *virkelig* fall within the same 'semantic field': both indicate a quality of being a good example of a kind. Each is used here to modify the noun 'princess', and one is also used to modify 'story'. So do the two adjectives differ subtly in meaning – more specifically, do they differ in meaning in this story? Secondly, what quality does the princess share with the story which allows both to be described as *rigtig*?

Looking in a dictionary will not help initially, because for both *rigtig* and *virkelig*, a dictionary will provide a selection of definitions (if it is monolingual) or translations (if it is bilingual) falling within the 'good example of its kind' field, most of which will work very well in each of the contexts in question. This is a reflection of the closeness in meaning of the two adjectives, of course, and it shifts the focus of inquiry sharply onto the second part of our first question: do the two adjectives differ in meaning *in this story*?

Clearly, neither a standard Danish corpus nor a standard Danish-English translation corpus will be especially useful in an attempt to answer this question. So where else might the translator look?

One answer would be: to other translators of this story. Translations of Hans Christian Andersen's stories into English have appeared regularly since the mid-1800s, so there is quite a corpus available, relatively speaking, and I present here (table 1) the solutions to the adjective problem provided by translators within the subcorpus consisting of copies that I have access to (see the list of Andersen translations in appendix):

| | |
|---|---|
| Anon | real princess (6); real princesses; true story |
| Blegvad | *real* princess; real princesses; real princess (5); a story |
| Corrin | *truly real* princess; *real* princesses; *real* princess (2); real princess (2); true princess; true story |
| Corrin/Corrin | *truly real* princess; *real* princesses; *real* princess (2); real princess (3); real story |
| De Chatelain | real princess; real ones; real princess (5); real story |
| Dulcken | *real* princess; real one; *real* princesses; real princess (4); true princess; true story |
| Hersholt | real one; real Princesses; real Princess (3); a Princess; real Princess; true story |

| Haugaard | real one; real princesses; real princess (4); real story |
| Kingsland | real princess (6); real princesses; true story |
| Lewis | real princess (5); the genuine article; fine story |
| Peachey | real Princess; real Princesses; real Princess (5); "Was not this a lady of real delicacy" |
| Peulevé | genuine Princess; real Princesses; real Princess (5); good story |
| Spink | *real* princess; real princesses; real princess (5); real story |
| Wehnert | real Princess; real Princesses; real Princess (5); true story |

**Table 1**. *rigtig* and *virkelig* in 14 English translations of Andersen's *Prindsesses paa Ærten* ("The princess on the pea")

It is not immediately obvious that this evidence is going to help us answer the questions we are concerned with (do *rigtig* and *virkelig* differ in meaning in this story and what property do the princess and the story share which makes both *rigtige*?): two translators, Corrin and Dulcken, distinguish between the adjectives and use one of them for the story as well as for the princess; Lewis and Peulevé also distinguish two adjectives for the princess, but have a third for the story; Anon, Blegvad, Hersholt, Kingsland and Wehnert distinguish in their adjective use between the princess and the story; Corrin and Corrin, De Chatelain, Haugaard, Peachey and Spink draw no distinction whatsoever. So the translator might reason that there is little point in paying particular attention to these two adjectives: any one or any pair that indicates something like a good example of its kind will do.

On the other hand, the discerning translator might treat this corpus, together with a dictionary, as providing guidance to potential equivalents, such as 'real', 'true', 'genuine' and 'fine', which could then be looked at in a monolingual corpus to see how they collocate. This would provide a lot of information which we do not have time to look at but which would, sadly, not enlighten the translator further. Each one would be fine, collocationally speaking, in almost any balance of allocation between princesses and stories. So where else could translators go?

Well, they could go to the rest of the writer's work in the fairytale genre. This constitutes a corpus which has the advantage of being truly representative: all that there is is all that there is. (Let us pass over quickly the possibility that it might still be misleading since a writer might change her lexical habits over a life time, so later date might skew the results regarding an early usage.)

The opus yields the following data (I report representative but select data, i.e. only data which do not raise additional questions to those currently in focus):

**From "The swineherd" (1842)**
"Fie Papa!" she said, "it is*n't* artificial, it is *virkelig*!"

**From "The nightingale" (1844)**
1. it was a little piece of artistry lying in a box, an artificial nightingale that was supposed to look like the live one but which was covered all over with diamonds, rubies and sapphires; as soon as it was wound up, the artificial bird could sing one of the pieces the *virkelig*e one sang,
2. the *virkelig*e nightingale sang in its own way, and the artificial bird was clockwork;
3. Then the artificial bird must sing alone. - It was as popular as the *virkelig*e one, and besides it was much prettier to look at: it glittered like bracelets and brooches.
4. that it [the artificial bird] was better than the *virkelig*e nightingale,
5. in the case of the *virkelig*e nightingale you can never predict what is going to happen, whereas in the case of the artificial bird, everything is arranged in advance!
6. But the poor fishermen who had heard the *virkelig*e nightingale said: "it [the artificial bird] sounds beautiful all right, and it does resemble it, but something is missing, I do*n't* know what!"

**From "The shepherdess and the chimney-sweep" (1845)**
Have you ever seen a *rigtig* old wooden cupboard, quite black with age and carved with intricate patterns of leaves?

**From "Holger Danske"(1845)**
"and here is a likeness of him!"
And it cast its shadow right up the wall, even a little way along the ceiling, it looked as if it was the *virkelig*e Holger Danske himself.

**From "The puck at the grocer's" (1853)**
There was a *rigtig* student, he lived in the attic and owned nothing; there was a *rigtig* grocer, he lived on the ground floor and owned the whole house.

In these data, *virkelig* is regularly opposed to terms indicating artificiality or artistry, and *rigtig* tends to indicate stereotypicality; this suggests that Andersen uses the adjectives *rigtig* and *virkelig* to distinguish between that which is genuinely and inherently what it purports to be, and that which either is a *stilleben* or (merely) conforms to socially held values, norms and expectations. Since this distinction is important thematically in the work, it might be useful in translations to seek to maintain support for it through lexical uses such as the adjective use we are currently contemplating. One solution might be to use e.g. *real* for *rigtig* and *genuine* for *virkelig*: according to the *Cobuild* dictionary (1987), something *real* (sense 2.1.) "has all the characteristics or qualities that such a thing typically has" whereas "something which is genuine is real and exactly what it appears to be, and is not fake or an imitation".

Obviously, in our focal story, this distinction is important: the prince is looking for the genuine article, as Naomi Lewis's translation has it (see above), but is rather unsure about how to recognize it when he sees it. The princess who presents herself claims to be it, but fails to conform to expectations on the surface and has to be tested. The test reveals that she possesses the sensitivity inherent in princesses. It is not clear that the prince, whose point of view predominates in the story, is any clearer towards the end about the difference, since the adjectives continue to be used for the princess in views attributed to him, and is the one he uses at the end ("he knew that he had a *rigtig* princess"); I take this to be a fine touch of irony. But it is significant that the princess herself claims to be *virkelig*, that it is this claim that the queen (who is the seat of wisdom in the story, who knows a test for princess-hood) sets out to test, and that it is this quality which is said to be possessed by the tender-skinned. And this is certainly a *real*, stereotypical story with the expected fairytale characters in it.

The problem we have just looked at was of course specific to a writer. But there are many translation problems which are idiosyncratic to one writer, so the idiosyncrasy problem itself is generic and in need of attention in translator education programmes. Perhaps trainees should be shown that it can be necessary to create specialized corpora (see also Johansson 1991) to help solve specialized problems, and a good way of showing this is to demonstrate that even the mighty standard corpora are not omnipotent.

I would now like to substantiate the claim I made above, that one of the assumptions underlying much use of corpora in pedagogy (that the linguistic future will and should resemble the past) is (only) a (pedagogically valuable) fiction, before turning to some consequences that follow from this.

# 4. On linguistic flux

The facts of linguistic flux are amply demonstrated historically: we are all familiar with notions like "Grimm's Law" or "the First Germanic Sound Shift" (Grimm 1822), and we know of changes that have taken place over time in the grammars and lexicons of languages too (see any work on historical linguistics; see also Adamson 1998, who describes a change in English grammar taking place in the 1990s in the use of the progressive). Furthermore, we know that we survive linguistically by being prepared for the future *not* to be like the past: we cope with idiolects, slips of the tongue, malapropisms, unfamiliar dialects and accents, and with linguistic innovation: the new metaphor or coinage which is also understood. As Davidson (1986) points out, the existence of linguistic never-befores shows that past experience only plays a part back-stage in linguistic encounters: it is a prop that helps users get by, but it is not what guarantees their success. What guarantees success is as minimal, though quite probably as firmly fixed in the human psyche as logical form is in language, namely speakers' abilities to agree on meanings from time to time. But this requires speakers to converge not towards past usage but towards the present, new use. Put philosophically (Davidson 1986: 166):

> the interpreter [hearer; *my gloss*] comes to the occasion of utterance with a theory that tells him (or so he believes) what an arbitrary utterance of the speaker means. The speaker then says something with the intention that it will be interpreted in a certain way, and the expectation that it will be so interpreted. In fact this way is not provided for by the interpreter's theory. But the speaker is nevertheless understood; the interpreter adjusts his theory so that it yields the speaker's intended interpretation.

Stated in a slightly more formal way, what happens is that the Speaker and Hearer both use (1) a prior theory and (2) a passing theory. The hearer's prior theory is a theory that expresses how he is prepared in advance to interpret the speaker. The speaker's prior theory expresses what she believes the hearer's prior theory to be. Prior theories take account of what the interactants know about each other, including what they might know about each other's speech behaviour from previous encounters, or encounters with people they take to be similar or different, and so on. It also includes knowledge about the immediate and general world of fact and discourse, including language. The prior theory for a speech encounter is a selection of all this kind of knowledge made on the basis of a judgement about what might be relevant (cf. Sperber and Wilson 1986) to the here and now. With practice and experience, people become increasingly skilled at selecting prior theories for various types of encounter with various types of interactant.

The passing theory is, for the speaker, the theory she intends the hearer to use. For the hearer, the passing theory is the theory he actually uses to interpret the utterance. Therefore, when communication succeeds, speaker and hearer converge on passing theories; not on prior theories. But neither theory is available fully fledged in advance of the encounter. Prior theories are already adjusted to each new encounter, so are not the same in all cases, and obviously, the passing theory is further adjusted (Davidson 1986: 173):

> As speaker and interpreter talk, their prior theories become more alike; so do their passing theories. The asymptote of agreement and understanding is when passing theories coincide. But the passing theory cannot in general correspond to an interpreter's linguistic competence [...]. Every deviation from ordinary usage, as long as it is agreed on for the moment... is in the passing theory as a feature of what the words mean on that occasion [...]. Of course things previously learned were essential to arriving at the passing theory, but what was learned could not have been the passing theory.

Meaning, on this view, is not an entity of some kind, which attaches to words or sentences, but a function from Speaker, Hearer, Utterance, Time, Place, Con- and Co-text, to an interpretation (Lewis 1970). The consequences for linguistics of this view can seem severe because they disturb the standard view of language as a fairly fixed system. On the other hand, it is possible to consider the view liberating, because it allows free movement between e.g. the literal and the figurative, and also between languages: a person's language will not get in the way of his or her ability to understand another person. All that is required is "the ability to converge on a passing theory from time to time" (Davidson 1986: 173). I think we should take this view to heart in both language teaching and translator education and use the evidence from corpora, at least some of the time, to demonstrate the novelty and inventiveness exhibited by translators.

This is especially important, because, where translation is concerned, the notion of language change is peculiarly complicated, meshing as it does with issues of linguistic borrowing, linguistic nationalism, linguistic authoritarianism, and the influence of one language on another, which can be particularly strongly felt in the case of translation. One of the reviewers of Peter Høeg's last novel (translated as *The Woman and the Ape* by Barbara Haveland (1996)), complains that the use of Danish in it is clearly styled for ease of translation, something which he finds deplorable (Skyum-Nielsen in *Information*, Friday 29 March 1996). I have not tried to examine the language of the original to establish whether I agree with the reviewer; the relevant point here is merely that he thinks such styling is a travesty. Many people object to the influence of one language on another and feel that the kind of innovation which can take place when translated texts import e.g. metaphors and idioms from the other language is thoroughly inappropriate. All the more reason, then, to try to empower young translators to take the plunge into linguistic inventiveness when this seems to them best to present what they want their writer to say in the language they are translating into. In the following section, I should like to demonstrate this need.

## 5.   Case study 2

Consider the following text extract:

> All of this Mads senses, at this moment, with the kind of clarity that follows a bad hangover or a long illness – not because he is clairvoyant but because he was born to the sensitivity and confusion of this century. And I know what I am talking about, because I am him – from now on you can call me Mads.

The extract is taken from pp 331-2 of Barbara Haveland's translation, *The History of Danish Dreams* (© 1995) (London: The Harvill Press, 1996) of Peter Høeg's *Forestilling om det tyvende århundrede* (Copenhagen: Munksgaard/Rosinante, 1988).

No non-Danish speaking, English speaking reader to whom I have shown this extract has found its final clause remarkable in any way (beyond finding the name a little strange, of course).

The Source Text for the extract is to be found on p. 334 of Høeg's
original, which I provide below together with an English gloss:

> og   alt dette føler Mads dette  øjeblik  med en klarhed  som
> and all  this  feels Mads this  moment  with a  clarity   like

> efter  svære tømmermænd eller lang    tids     sygdom,
> after  a severe hangover       or   a long  time's  illness,

> og  det er ikke fordi han  er clairvoyant men fordi  han
> and it  is  not  because he  is clairvoyant but because he

> er født til dette århundredes følsomhed og  forvirring,
> is born to this  century's   sensitivity and confusion,

> og jeg ved hvad  jeg  taler om,         for    det er
> and I  know what   I     am talking about, because    it is

> mig der er  ham, fra   nu   af  kan Ikalde mig Mads,
> I   who am  he, from now on  can  you call    me  Mads.

As the gloss shows, the translation is remarkably close to the source
text; and in the case of the last clause, the only departure from the Source
Text made in the Target Text is one demanded by English grammar. Yet
the Source Text contains a figure of speech of the kind which might be
thought likely to send translators scurrying to their dictionary of idioms
to find an expressions with a different surface form than the Source Text
expression but conveying what could be thought of as the 'same meaning': when one Dane declares to another a willingness to be called Mads,
s/he is doing what an English speaker would be doing in declaring him or
herself to be *the Queen of Sheba*. In other words, by saying: "If x, then
you can call me Mads", a Dane will be indicating that x is not the case;
and as this extract comes very near the end of the novel, Høeg is drawing
on the figure of speech to emphasize the fictional nature of all that has
gone before. Obviously, "from now on you can call me Mads" does not
do this for readers of the Target Text unless they know Danish. But equally
obviously, "from now on you can call me the Queen of Sheba" would sit
rather badly in the context of the rest of the text extract, and Haveland has
chosen to use instead the English expression which most straightforwardly
matches the Source Text expression word for word. Not very creative,

one might feel, and liable to lead to a so-called 'loss' in translation. But I would argue the opposite: that Haveland's choice is highly creative and that all that is lost in the Target Text, if anything, is a little touch of local irony that the expression "fra nu af kan I kalde mig Mads" endows the Source Text with, but which "from now on you can call me Mads" fails to provide in the Target Text. My justification for these claims derives from a consideration of the situation of the Target Text clause in the context of the whole novel.

The fictional nature of the story that the book tells is never really in doubt, of course, since the book is sold as a novel. Its title, *The History of Danish Dreams* further signals that the history to be recounted may be less than factual, and this impression is further and continually reinforced from the moment reading begins. The history begins in 1520, although the main character in Part I, Carl Laurids, is said to have been born, probably, on New Year's Eve 1900, on a country estate, Mørkhøj, where time has stood still for at least 200 years on the order of the Count of Mørkhøj, who is convinced that the centre of the universe is to be found on his estate. The Count invites a number of scholars to a ceremony during which the centre of the universe is to be revealed. The attending scholars include, among others, Casper Bartholin (1585-1629) and Ole Rømer (1644-1710), whose dates of birth and death, along with brief bibliographies, can be found in a list at the back of the book of 'real-life' characters who populate the book along with the fictional characters that English readers cannot be assumed to be familiar with because they figure large only in Danish history.

As mentioned above, the passage we are concerned with is taken from near the end of the story, and in it, one of the non-historical (fictional) characters, Mads, suddenly reveals himself to be the narrator. I think that the translation of this novel as a whole provides the English reader with sufficiently strong hints about the text genre for them to react appropriately to this revelation that Mads is the narrator of the history of his own family, even though they might miss the local touch of irony which the Danish reader is afforded at this point by the use of the Danish phrase.

# 6.  Conclusion and a final caution

I think that Haveland's solution to the problem presented by the text extract above is brilliant; and it seems to me that one thing (among many others, of course) that student translators could do with in addition to strategies to help them avoid pitfalls is encouragement to dare to achieve the brilliant – for there is no doubt that it takes both courage and experience to translate as Haveland has done here. But, paradoxically, if one day Haveland's translation with its Source Text were to enter a corpus of Danish-English translations it would have the potential to mislead scores of future translators, who might come across this expression in contexts very unlike the present one and for which Haveland's translation might not be successful. Naturally, learners will be warned that if there is only one instance of a pairing in a corpus, they should follow the model it shows them with caution. But they should also be told that beneath this blanket caution against *copying* 'dangerous' models lies a deeper lesson, crucial to fostering excellence in translation: sometimes it is necessary to break a norm instead of obeying it. The trick is knowing when, and that is one thing we cannot learn from a corpus. The most we can hope for from a corpus in this connection is a measure of the power of the rogue translation provided by the mass of standard-translation counterexamples; but then that might very well be worth having.

# References

Adamson, Sylvia (1998) 'The Code as Context: Language-change and (Mis)Interpretation', in Kirsten Malmkjær and John Williams (eds) *Context in Language Learning and Language Understanding*, Cambridge: Cambridge University Press, 137-168.

Baker, Mona (1995) 'Corpora in Translation Studies: An Overview and Some Suggestions for Future Research', *Target* 7(2): 223-243.

------ (1996) 'Corpus-based Translation Studies: The Challenges that Lie Ahead', in Harold Somers (ed) *Terminology, LSP and Translation: Studies in Language Engineering, in Honour of Juan C. Sager*, Amsterdam and Philadelphia: John Benjamins, 175-186.

Chomsky, Noam (1995) *The Minimalist Program*, Cambridge, Mass.: The MIT Press.

Davidson, Donald (1986) 'A Nice Derangement of Epitaphs', in Ernest Lepore (ed) *Truth and Interpretation: Perspectives on the Philosophy of Donald Davidson*, Oxford: Basil Blackwell, 433-446. Also in Richard Grandy and Richard Warner (eds) (1986) *Philosophical Grounds of Rationality: Intentions, Categories, Ends*, Oxford: Clarendon Press, 157-174.

Grimm, Jacob (1822) *Deutche Grammatik*, Göttingen; also 1893, Gütersloh: Bertelmann.

Johansson, Stig (1991) 'Times Change and so Do Corpora', in Karin Aijmer and Bengt Altenberg (eds) *English Corpus Linguistics: Studies in Honour of Jan Svartvik*, London and New York: Longman, 305-314.

Knowles, Murray and Kirsten Malmkjær (1991) 'Key Terms in H. C. Andersen's Fairytales and their Translations into English', *Babel* 37(4): 203-212.

Laviosa, Sara (1998) 'The English Comparable Corpus: A Resource and a Methodology', in Lynne Bowker, Michæl Cronin, Dorothy Kenny and Jennifer Pearson (eds) *Unity in Diversity? Current Trends in Translation Studies*. Manchester: St. Jerome, 101-112.

Lewis, David (1970) 'General Semantics', *Synthese* 22: 18-67.

Malmkjær, Kirsten (1993) 'Who Can Make *Nice* a Better Word Than *Pretty*: Collocation, Translation and Psycholinguistics', in Mona Baker, Gill Francis and Elena Tognini-Bonelli (eds) *Text and Technology: In Honour of John Sinclair*, Amsterdam and Philadelphia: John Benjamins, 213-232.

------ (1995) 'What's in an Adjective', *Norwich Papers in European Languages, Literatures and Culture* 3: 44-54.

*Meta* (1998) 'L'approche Basée sur le Corpus/The Corpus-based Approach', Special Issue 43(4).

Sinclair, John (1991) *Corpus, Concordance, Collocation,* Oxford: Oxford University Press.

------ and Antoinette Renouf (1988) 'A Lexical Syllabus for Language Learning', in Ronald Carter and Michæl McCarthy (eds) *Vocabulary and Language Teaching*, London and New York: Longman, 140-158.

Sperber, Dan and Deirdre Wilson (1986) *Relevance: Cognition and Context* (second edition 1995), Oxford: Basil Blackwell.

Toury, Gideon (1980) 'Translated Literature: System, Norm, Performance: Toward a TT-oriented Approach to Literary Translation', in *In Search of a Theory of Translation*, Tel Aviv, Tel Aviv University, The Porter Institute for Poetics and Semiotics, 35-50. Reprinted in: *Poetics Today* (1981), 2:4, 9-27.

Zanettin, Federico (1998) 'Bilingual Comparable Corpora and the Training of Translators', *Meta* 43(4): 616-30.

# Appendix

Hans Christian Andersen translations referred to in the text:

*Danish Fairy Legends and Tales*. Caroline Peachey, London: William Pickering, 1846. Second, enlarged edition, 1852.

*Tales and Fairy Stories*. Madame de Chatelain, London: Routledge & Co, 1852

*Andersen's Tales for Children*. Wehnert, Alfred, London: Bell & Daldy, 1861

*Stories and Tales*. Henry William Dulcken, London: Routledge, 1864

*What the Moon Saw, and Other Tales*. Henry William Dulcken, London: Routledge, 1865

*Hans Christian Andersen's Stories for the Household.* H.W. Dulcken, London: Routledge, 1866. Re-issued as *The Complete Illustrated Works of Hans Christian Andersen.* London, Chancellor Press, 1983; 1994.

*The Complete Andersen: All of the 168 Stories by Hans Christian Andersen.* Jean Hersholt. New York: Limited Editions Club 1942-47. Available in electronic form on MAGNUS, from CD-Danmark A/S, Palægade 4, P.O. Box 9026, DK-1022 Copenhagen K, Denmark.

*Eighty Fairy Tales.* Translated by R.P. Keigwin. Odense: Skandinavisk Bogforlag. 1976. With an introduction by Elias Bredsdorff, New York: Pantheon Books, 1982 (This translation first published by Flensted (Denmark) in 1950).

*Hans Christian Andersen. Fairy Tales and Stories. Translated, with an Introduction, by Reginald Spink.* London, 1960. Republished in the series Everyman's Library Children's Classics, London 1992.

*The Complete Fairy Tales and Stories.* Translated from the Danish by Erik Christian Haugaard. Foreword by Naomi Lewis. London: Gollanz, 1974. Also published, with a foreword by Virginia Haviland, New York, Doubleday & Co. New Edition, Gollancz Children's Paperbacks, 1994.

*Hans Christian Andersen. Stories and Fairy Tales Selected, Translated and Illustrated by Erik Blegvad.* London, 1993.

# Reflections on Corpora
# and their Uses in Cross-linguistic Research

STIG JOHANSSON

*The paper attempts to set up a framework within which the contributions in the book can be interpreted, and surveys some recent developments in the compilation and use of corpora for cross-linguistic research and translation studies. Research questions and applications are considered, and different models for the building of multilingual corpora are presented, with particular reference to recent work at the University of Oslo. The paper stresses that corpora provide openings both for learning and research. Access to corpora may even help to bring learning and research together. This is an auspicious time to focus on corpus use and learning to translate.*

## 1.  Introduction

The starting-point for this paper was my summing-up talk at the end of the second conference on "Corpus Use and Learning to Translate" (*CULT 2K*). The title alludes to a visionary paper written by John Sinclair some twenty years ago (Sinclair 1982) when corpora were limited in size, range, and use. In the course of the last two decades the size and range of corpora have grown enormously, and it is now widely recognized that they have many uses both in research and teaching. One such use, which is receiving increasing attention and which has been stimulated by the *CULT* conferences, is the application of corpora to translation studies.

## 2.  The changing nature of corpora

In his (1982) paper John Sinclair draws a distinction between relatively small sample corpora, such as the million-word *Brown* and *LOB* corpora, and monitor corpora which can hold a state of the language for research purposes and change with the language. Now the 100-millon-word *British National Corpus* and the even larger *Bank of English* are available, not to mention the almost unlimited availability of texts on the Internet. Just as striking is the extension of the types of texts available for computer analysis. There has been a quantum leap both in terms of size and range.

As implied by the idea of monitor corpora, a corpus is no longer necessarily conceived as something limited and permanent. In some cases corpora can be composed on the fly by selecting from the vast amount of texts available, taking into account the research problem or the intended application. And, in the words of Krista Varantola (this volume), they can even be disposable, i.e. designed to be thrown away after the task is completed.

Although corpora can be disposable, I will mainly be concerned with carefully crafted corpora, and particularly with corpora designed to be more long-lasting tools for cross-linguistic research and translation studies. We can distinguish between two main types:

- corpora of comparable original texts in two or more languages;
- corpora of original texts and their translations into one or more other languages.

The two types are not mutually exclusive, but complementary, and they can even be combined within the same overall framework (see Section 4 below). McEnery and Baker (this volume) make the important point that there is a need to extend the genres of multilingual corpora and to build multilingual corpora that include a wider range of languages.

Before we go into more detail as regards the types of corpora designed for cross-linguistic research and translation studies, let us briefly consider relevant research questions and applications, because it is these which must guide the building of corpora.

## 3. Research questions and applications

John Sinclair ends his paper by suggesting that corpora will "allow new kinds of access to the patterns of the language", patterns which are "inaccessible to direct observation" (Sinclair 1982: 6). This is true not least of an area that has been close to his heart, viz. collocations (dealt with at length in Sinclair 1991). There should be no need to go into the ways in which monolingual corpora have enriched the study of individual languages in lexis, grammar, discourse, language variation, etc.

The study of multilingual corpora throws the characteristics of the individual languages into relief, and makes it possible to map correspondences between languages in great detail. Whereas contrastive studies in the past were often limited to a comparison of language systems in the abstract, we can now compare and contrast languages in use, including stylistic preferences and quantitative patterns.

If our interest is in general aspects of language(s), multilingual corpora are equally useful. The comparison may reveal both features which are unique and characteristics which are more or less generally shared by languages. In other words, multilingual corpora have a role to play both in contrastive analysis, which tends to focus on differences between pairs of languages, and in language typology and the study of universals, which necessarily include a broader range of languages.

In his paper on "A translational basis for semantics" Helge Dyvik stresses the importance of bringing a multilingual perspective into the study of semantics, and he points out that:

> [...] translation is one of the very few cases where speakers evaluate meaning relations between expressions without doing so as part of some metalinguistic, philosophical or theoretical reflection, but as a normal kind of linguistic activity. (Dyvik 1998: 51)

Translation serves as a semantic mirror, reflecting meanings across languages, and the images can be studied through multilingual corpora. The correspondences established by skilled bilinguals in the translation process help us map the relationships between languages. Dyvik goes beyond this, however, in claiming that the study of translation may play a role in laying the foundations of linguistic semantics.

Multilingual corpora are useful not just for language description, but specifically for the study of translation. A corpus of original texts and translations can be a rich source in the study of translation patterns, not least for those who are learning to translate. They can learn by observing how professional translators have dealt with problems of lexis and grammar, idioms, colloquialisms, culture-specific references, etc. And those who are engaged in bilingual lexicography or (semi-)automatic translation will do well to consult corpora showing the work of professional translators.

If we want to use multilingual corpora for all these purposes and avoid the well-known pitfalls (translators make mistakes, each translation is only one of a number of possible translations, translation is a special text type which does not adequately represent the target language, and so on; cf. Ebeling 2000: 25ff), there are advantages in choosing a framework like the one we adopted for the *English-Norwegian Parallel Corpus* (Johansson and Hofland 1994, Johansson 1998; for an update on the project, see: http://www.hf.uio.no/iba/prosjekt/).

# 4.  Bi-directional translation corpora

The *English-Norwegian Parallel Corpus* can be described as a bi-directional translation corpus. It consists of original texts in each language and their translations into the other language: English to Norwegian and Norwegian to English. The texts are matched as regards number and extent, approximate time of publication, and text type. To reduce the influence of idiosyncratic features, a consistent attempt was made to include a wide range of authors and translators. Similar corpora have been compiled for English-Swedish and English-Finnish within the framework of the Nordic project "Languages in Contrast". Other related projects focus on language pairs such as French-Norwegian, Estonian-Swedish, English-German, and English-Portuguese (see the paper by Ana Frankenberg-Garcia and Diana Santos, this volume).

Because such corpora are bi-directional, we can study translation patterns going from either language and in either direction, i.e. we can identify correspondences going from the original to the target language (how has X been translated?), or we can start from the target language and see what correspondences we can establish (what is the source of X?).

In a paper on sentence connectors in the *English-Swedish Parallel Corpus*, Bengt Altenberg (1999) outlines an approach to the study of correspondences in a bi-directional translation corpus. It is possible to set up a scale of mutual correspondence where, for example, we find English *instead* and its closest Swedish translation equivalent *i stället* high up, and *however* and *emellertid* considerably lower down. The correspondence between the last two is asymmetric. While *emellertid* is translated by *however* in the great majority of cases, *however* is often translated by other connectors than *emellertid*. Needless to say, such results are insufficient without an interpretation, but we cannot go into detail here. Altenberg goes on to show how the approach can be extended beyond single lexical items to subsystems in the two languages.

The main advantage of a bi-directional translation corpus of this kind is that we get a subcorpus of comparable original texts into the bargain. The subcorpus can be used as the basis for contrastive studies. Alternatively, we can use it to check findings based on a comparison of original texts and translations. If the results agree, we can be confident that they correctly reflect the relationship between the languages. If they disagree, we may assume that we have identified characteristics that have to do with translation.

To reveal features which are characteristic of translation, we can focus on another dimension of comparison which is included in the overall framework: comparing original and translated texts in the same language (for both of the languages included). Finally, we can compare translated texts in the two languages, to reveal general aspects of translated language.

To sum up, we could say that the overall framework allows a comparison across a number of dimensions. The corpus changes, so to speak, depending upon our perspective and according to the focus of the study. There is an important limitation, however. To build a corpus of this kind, we need comparable types of texts which have been translated in both directions. In the case of English and Norwegian, the task turned out to be feasible, in spite of the fact that translations from English into Norwegian are far more numerous and much more varied than those in the opposite direction. For other language pairs, it may be more problematic, or even impossible. In our own case, we recognize that the bi-directional translation corpus has to be supplemented by larger monolingual corpora to adequately represent the texts in each language.

## 5. Diamonds and stars

If we are interested in language or translation more generally, it is desirable to include more languages and build a truly multilingual corpus. At present, we are attempting to extend the corpus model outlined above to three languages: English, German, and Norwegian (see the web page for the trilingual project: http://www.hf.uio.no/german/sprik/). In other words, the corpus is intended to include comparable original texts in the three languages, together with translations into the other two languages: English to German and Norwegian; German to English and Norwegian; Norwegian to English and German.

Figure 1 shows the model in the form of a diagram – we have christened it the diamond model (the figure was first drawn in this way by my colleague Cathrine Fabricius-Hansen). It incorporates exactly the same types of dimensions as the original two-language model (as presented, for example, in Johansson 1998). In other words, we can compare:

- original texts in the three languages;
- original texts and translations across the languages;
- original and translated texts in the same language;
- translated texts across the languages.

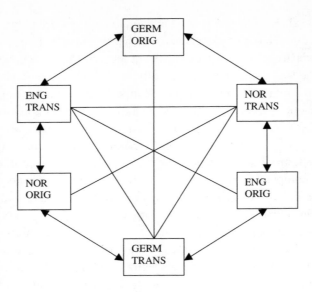

**Figure 1.** Multidimensional analysis of English, German, and Norwegian

The problem mentioned at the end of Section 4 gets even more serious in this case. To what extent can we find comparable texts that have been translated across the three languages? It is likely that the trilingual corpus will remain incomplete, but even if the project succeeds only in part, it will have been worthwhile.

Another multilingual model is shown in Figure 2 – we could call it the star model. We have collected translations of a number of our English original texts into three languages apart from Norwegian: German, Dutch, and Portuguese. As many of the English original texts are shared with our Swedish and Finnish sister projects, we can then compare across six languages using English as a point of departure. In the comparison, we hope to uncover general features of translation as well as language-specific translation patterns. Characteristics of the individual languages will be highlighted. Basically the same approach, with different texts and different languages, is used in Wolfgang Teubert's work (e.g. 1999) on cross-linguistic correspondences.

The star model can also be applied to multiple translations into the same target language of the same original text(s). At the University of Oslo we have commissioned translations of two texts – a short story and a scientific article – from some of the best and most experienced translators in Norway. There were ten translators for each text, and each translator

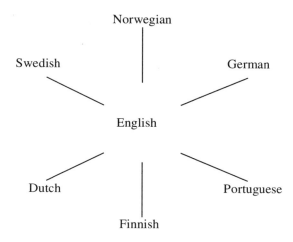

**Figure 2.** The star model: English original and translations

handed in a draft version and a final edited version. The texts had not been translated before, and the translators worked independently of each other. The intention of the project is to study the extent and types of variation in translation in an attempt to uncover translation norms. In addition, the material is well suited for translation teaching. Students can be asked to translate part of the texts and can later compare, and discuss, the ways in which problems have been handled by the students and the professional translators.

The interesting paper by Kirsten Malmkjær (this volume) on translations of Hans Christian Andersen can be regarded as representing the star model, though in this case the translations were made at different times, and we must assume that later translators have often been familiar with the earlier versions. A corpus of this kind of material should be excellent as well in the teaching of translation. And, I might add, a corpus of translations does not necessarily have to contain texts by a range of authors or derive from a range of sources – it can be author-specific or text-specific.

The star model can also, at least partly, be applied to collections of student translations (see the paper by Lynne Bowker and Peter Bennison, this volume), as groups of students are normally asked to translate the same text. Ideally, such a corpus should also include model translations, with variants, so that students can compare their own work with the model. A translation archive and student tracking system, above all, provides the opportunity – important for both teachers and learners – to identify recurrent translation problems and to track the development of the individual student.

My survey does not give an exhaustive account of relevant types of corpora and their uses in cross-linguistic research and translation studies. A very interesting type contains texts that have been produced under conditions of parallel writing in different languages (see Gunnarsson *et al.* 1999: 28ff.). In this case, there is not really a source text, but rather a specific task or some central ideas, and both the form and content of the text (e.g. an advertisement) are adapted to the target audience. There is no finite number of types of corpora, nor is there any limit (aside from one's imagination) to the range of possible research questions and applications.

## 6. Learning and research

One of the most fascinating aspects of corpora is that they provide a good basis both for learning and research. Translation teachers and researchers will find many ideas in this book. Corpora provide an excellent means of consciousness-raising for learners or, to use the expression of Stella Tagnin (2002), of training the innocent translator. The focus of corpus studies can be more narrowly linguistic, e.g. to do with terminology (Belinda Maia, this volume) or collocations, or on the wider issues of cultural adaptation, as in the paper in this volume by Jennifer Pearson. Suggestions for the integration of corpora in translation training are given in Natalie Kübler's paper.

Though corpora are most often used to uncover general patterns, they also provide a treasury for the study of creative language use. Just compare a typical entry in a bilingual dictionary with what you can find in a corpus-based bilingual concordance; the latter provides a far richer set of correspondences. As Allén (1992: 1) puts it, in authentic texts we find both the *ostinato* and the *capriccio* of language.

Access to corpora may contribute to a narrowing of learning and research. Learners who work with corpora can be given more challenging tasks than with many traditional language exercises. As suggested in this book, they may even be trained to compile a corpus to solve a particular task. Learning becomes a form of research, far from rote learning. And there is just a short step in moving on to the real world of language use and new translation tasks, with a sharpened sense of observation, prepared to meet the unknown.

# 7. Conclusions

In discussions with practising translators about our work on multilingual corpora it is far from easy to get the message across. This is probably because translators are more concerned with individual texts, and specifically with problems to do with idioms, culture-specific vocabulary, and the like. Corpus investigations, on the other hand, tend to focus on patterns that go beyond the individual text (though not necessarily so: cf. Sections 5 and 6). In my view it needs to be impressed upon translators that such patterns are relevant and interesting: they can reveal, for example, how skilled translators have approached texts, confronted problems and discovered solutions. Now it might be argued that expecting a professional translator to take an interest in corpus research is rather like asking an author to read works on linguistics – certainly ambitious and perhaps irrelevant too. Yet there is no doubt that *CULT* has formulated an important task: "Corpus Use and Learning to Translate". Translation has to be learned, even by those fortunate individuals who have grown up with more than one language.

Now is a good time to focus on the use of corpora in translation training. Corpora of different kinds, both monolingual and multilingual, are available in plenty, and others can be compiled on the fly using the Internet. Tools for working with multilingual corpora are being developed, and interest would appear to be growing both among teachers and researchers.

In 1977, when computer corpus studies were still in their infancy, a new corpus enterprise began: *ICAME* – the *International Computer Archive of Modern English* (now: the *International Computer Archive of Modern and Medieval English*). This has served as a channel of contact for an increasing number of researchers. New projects have been initiated, often involving collaboration between teams of researchers. Some years ago we saw the start of another successful initiative, *TaLC: Teaching and Language Corpora*. *CULT* is now taking the lead in the field of corpora and learning to translate. There are plenty of tasks ahead. I will mention just one: creating multilingual diamonds and stars (cf. Section 5). This can hardly be undertaken without cooperation.

All in all, the papers presented at the second conference on Corpus Use and Learning to Translate have shown that, when used with insight and imagination, corpora can be a versatile, rewarding and motivating resource, of crucial importance in translator education.

# References

Allén, Sture (1992) 'Opening Address', in Jan Svartvik (ed) *Directions in Corpus Linguistics. Proceedings of Nobel Symposium 82, Stockholm, 4-8 August 1991*, Berlin and New York: Mouton de Gruyter, 1-3.

Altenberg, Bengt (1999) 'Adverbial Connectors in English and Swedish: Semantic and Lexical Correspondences', in Hilde Hasselgård and Signe Oksefjell (eds), *Out of Corpora: Studies in Honour of Stig Johansson*, Amsterdam and Atlanta, GA: Rodopi, 249-268.

Dyvik, Helge (1998) 'A Translational Basis for Semantics', in Stig Johansson and Signe Oksefjell (eds) *Corpora and Cross-linguistic Research: Theory, Method, and Case Studies*, Amsterdam and Atlanta, GA: Rodopi, 51-86.

Ebeling, Jarle (2000) *Presentative Constructions in English and Norwegian: A Corpus-based Contrastive Study*, Acta Humaniora 68, Oslo: Unipub forlag.

Gunnarsson, B-L, C. Johansson, K. Jämtelid, A.S. Skulstad, B. Norlyk, and A-M Bülow-Møller (1999) 'The Study of Discourse in Organizations', in Päivi Pietilä and Olli-Pekka Salo (eds) *Multiple Languages – Multiple Perspectives: Texts on Language Teaching and Linguistic Research*. AFinLA Yearbook 1999. Publications de l'Association Finlandaise de Linguistique Appliquée 57, Jyväskylä, 9-54.

Johansson, Stig (1998) 'On the Role of Corpora in Cross-linguistic Research', in Stig Johansson and Signe Oksefjell (eds) *Corpora and Cross-linguistic Research: Theory, Method, and Case Studies*, Amsterdam and Atlanta, GA: Rodopi, 3-24.

------ and Knut Hofland (1994) 'Towards an English-Norwegian Parallel Corpus', in Udo Fries, Gunnel Tottie and Peter Schneider (eds) *Creating and Using English Language Corpora*. Amsterdam and Atlanta, GA: Rodopi, 25-37.

Sinclair, John (1982) 'Reflections on Computer Corpora in English Language Research', in Stig Johansson (ed) *Computer Corpora in English Language Research*, Bergen: Norwegian Computing Centre for the Humanities, 1-6.

------ (1991) *Corpus, Concordance, Collocation*, Oxford: Oxford University Press.

Tagnin, Stella (2002) 'Corpora and the Innocent Translator: How Can They Help Him?', *InTRAlinea* 5, online: www.intralinea.it.

Wolfgang, Teubert (1999) 'Corpus Linguistics: A Partisan View', online: http://tractor.bham.ac.uk/ijcl/teubert_cl.html.

# Notes on Contributors

**Paul Baker** is a research associate in the Department of Linguistics and Modern English Language, Lancaster University. He has worked on a range of corpus building projects, including the *BNC*. His most recent research in corpus linguistics has been in the area of exploring and meeting the needs for corpus data of non-indigenous minority languages in the UK.

**Peter Bennison** holds a degree in Computer Science and is a software developer with over ten years of experience developing computer tools in the telecommunications, financial, and language engineering sectors.

**Silvia Bernardini** teaches translation and linguistics at the School for Interpreters and Translators of the University of Bologna at Forlì, Italy. For the past three years she has been involved in the construction of the CEXI corpus, a parallel bi-directional corpus of English and Italian.

**Lynne Bowker** holds degrees in Translation and Language Engineering and has been involved in translator training since 1995. Formerly employed at Dublin City University in Ireland, she now teaches at the University of Ottawa in Canada. She is a certified translator with the Association of Translators and Interpreters of Ontario. Her research interests include translation pedagogy, corpus-based translation and computer-assisted translation.

**Ana Frankenberg-Garcia** is an Auxiliary Professor in the Translation Department at the Instituto Superior de Línguas e Administração, Lisbon. She holds a B.A. in History from the University of São Paulo and a Ph.D. in Applied Linguistics from the University of Edinburgh. Her doctoral dissertation is on second language academic writing. Her current research interests include second language learning, translation, contrastive linguistics and crosslinguistic influence applied to Portuguese and to English. She is responsible for *Compara*, the Portuguese-English Parallel Corpus.

**Stig Johansson** is Professor of Modern English Language at the Department of British and American Studies, University of Oslo, Norway. He has been involved in the compilation and analysis of the *LOB* Corpus, the *English-Norwegian Parallel Corpus*, and the *Oslo Multilingual Corpus*.

He was co-ordinating secretary of *ICAME* for many years and editor of the *ICAME Journal*. His publications include (as editor and contributor) *Computer Corpora in English Language Research* (1982), (as editor, together with Signe Oksefjell, and as contributor) *Corpora and Cross-linguistic Research: Theory, Method, and Case Studies* (1998), and (with Douglas Biber, Geoffrey Leech, Susan Conrad, and Edward Finegan) *Longman Grammar of Spoken and Written English* (1999).

**Natalie Kübler** is an associate professor at the University of Paris 7 in the Department of Intercultural Studies and Applied Languages. She currently teaches linguistics, corpus linguistics and its applications in translation and terminology. She wrote her PhD on automated error correction of grammatical errors made by French speakers in English, under the supervision of professor Maurice Gross LADL, University of Paris 7. She has participated in a university project for the second language grammar checker ARCTA at the Language and Speech Processing Laboratory, University of Neuchâtel, Switzerland. Recent research focuses on the integration of corpora in Web-based CALL and terminology extraction in French and English; another research direction consists in studying the Swiss variety of French on Swiss-French corpora.

**Belinda Maia** is an auxiliary professor at the University of Porto where she has worked since 1974. During this period she has taught a variety of subjects including English Language and Culture, Contemporary Culture, Translation Theory, Contrastive Linguistics, Translation and Information Technology applied to Translation. She has also given Master's degree seminars in "Linguistics and Translation" and "Information Technology and Translation". Her research interests are in the area of contrastive linguistics, terminology and the application of language technologies to research and translation practice.

**Kirsten Malmkjær** is Professor of Translation Studies and Director of the Centre for Research in Translation at Middlesex University in London, UK.

**Tony McEnery** is Head of Department at the Department of Linguistics, Lancaster University. He has published widely on corpus based language study and has developed corpora in a range of languages over the past decade.

**Jennifer Pearson** is Chief of Translation at UNESCO Headquarters in

Paris. Previously, she was senior lecturer in translation and corpus linguistics in the School of Applied Language and Intercultural Studies at Dublin City University. Author of *Terms in Context* (John Benjamins, 1998); co-author (with Lynne Bowker) of *Working with specialized language: a practical introduction to using corpora* (Routledge, 2002); co-editor of *Bibliography of Translation Studies* (St. Jerome Publishing 1998, 1999, 2000, 2001) and of *Translation Studies: Unity in Diversity?* (St. Jerome Publishing 1998). Formerly, director of the National Centre for Language Technology and manager of Ireland's Eurotra (EU funded MT project) team (1988-1992). Staff translator/interpreter with the Irish Export Board, 1980-1984.

**Diana Santos** is a researcher at *SINTEF Telecom and Informatics*, Oslo. She has worked with natural language processing since 1987. She graduated in Electrical Engineering and Computers at the Instituto Superior Técnico (Technical University of Lisbon) in 1985. At the same university, she wrote her MSc thesis on English-into-Portuguese machine translation (1988) and her PhD thesis on corpus-based contrastive semantics (1996). Her main research areas are corpus processing, translation and evaluation, but she has also worked in parsing, spelling checking, computer-aided lexicography and speech coding. She is head of the *Computational Processing of Portuguese* project.

**Dominic Stewart** holds a PhD in Italian Linguistics from the University of Reading, and teaches linguistics and translation at the School for Interpreters and Translators of the University of Bologna at Forlì, Italy. His current research interests focus on the use of large general language corpora in language learning and translation training.

**Krista Varantola** is professor of English at the Department of Translation Studies, University of Tampere. She has published widely on language for special purposes and on dictionary use in translation. Her current research interests are the use of electronic text corpora in translation, interactive electronic dictionaries, as well as interactive lexical interfaces to knowledge bases – in other words, the creation of human-driven technology (software) and not technology-driven humans.

**Federico Zanettin** is Research Fellow in Applied Linguistics at the Università per Stranieri of Perugia, Italy. He holds a Doctorate in Translation

Studies (Bologna) and has taught translation and computer assisted translation courses at the School for Translators and Interpreters of the University of Bologna at Forlì, Italy. His main research interests are translation studies, corpus linguistics, multimedia and intercultural communication. He is editor of the online translation journal *inTRAlinea* (http://www.intralinea.it).

# Index

Gujarati                        91, 98
Gunnarsson, B.-L.                    142

Halliday, MAK                        46
Haugaard, Erik C.                    124
Haveland, Barbara    8, 129, 131-132
Hebrew                            93, 95
Hersholt, Jean                    123-124
Hindi                          91, 93, 98
*History of Danish Dreams,*
    *The (Forestilling om det*
    *tyvende århundrede)*    129, 131
Høeg, Peter            8, 129-130
Hofland, Knut                        137
Holger Danske                        125
Holmes, James S.                      1
Howcroft, Susan                  46, 47
HTML (HyperText Markup
    Language)    26-27, 32-34, 83

*ICAME* (Modern English
    International Computer
    Archive of Modern and
    Medieval English)            143
*IMS Corpus Workbench*    71, 77,
                                  81-82
information retrieval            43, 62
ISO standards                        50

Japanese                          90, 93
*Java*                              116
Johansson, Stig        8, 71, 75, 126,
                            135, 137, 139
Johns, Tim                    4, 10, 83
Jull Costa, Margaret                 79

Kenny, Dorothy                  3, 5, 11
Khouri, Liliane                      89
Kingsland, L. W.                     124
Kiraly, Don                           5
knowledge management            57, 59
Knowles, Murray                      121
Kordoni, Valia                        90

Kübler, Natalie    10, 25, 28, 29, 39,
                                  142
*KWIC* (Key-Word-In-Context)    83

language learning            2, 82, 104
language teaching          2, 5, 128
Laviosa, Sara        2, 17, 104, 119
Lefevere, André                      58
Lewis, David                        128
Lewis, Naomi                    124, 126
*LOB Corpus*                        135
localisation              3, 26, 41, 61
Lodge, David                      73, 79
LSP                    25, 35, 43, 46
*Lúcio's Confession*                 79

*Macintosh*                        106
*Madame Bovary*                     79
Maia, Belinda        7, 28, 43, 142
Malmkjær, Kirsten        3, 8, 10, 11,
                        78, 119, 121, 141
Martin, James                        46
McEnery, Tony    4, 8, 46, 89, 91,
                        97, 102, 136
*Meta*                              119
*Microsoft Access*    33, 94, 108, 110
*Microsoft Word*        94, 106-107
*MILLE* (Minority Language
    Engineering)    89, 91, 98-100
*Minmark*                            17
*MonoConc*                    108, 110
MT (Machine Translation)        3, 28,
                    33, 35, 39, 41, 56, 97
*MULTEXT* (Multilingual Text
    Tools and Corpora)            89
*MULTEXT East* (Multilingual
    Text Tools and Corpora for
    Central and Eastern
    European Languages)            90
*Multiconcord*                      18

NLP (Natural Language
    Processing)    8, 26, 27, 28, 42